# On My Way Up

By

## Alyson Kirk

For John, the love of my life.
May we pursue our passions
through new adventures
until the day we die.

**In memory of**
**Christian Pruchnic — Gone too soon**
**Climber, Runner, Guide, Mentor, Best Friend**

# On My Way UP

# Part One

## Rosalie

Colorado's 13,575-foot Rosalie Peak
Photo by John Kirk

# Prologue

I'd heard that freezing and bleeding to death were the easiest ways to die. There would be numbness, and a person would simply fall asleep. *Whoever said that never lay on a snow-covered mountain, freezing and bleeding to death.* There was no numbness or sleep—only torture. Dying was not easy.

A moment before my fall, I could never have imagined the gut-wrenching despair and hopelessness that would soon wash over me. I squirmed in agony, but every move brought on fresh waves of torture. Each time I shivered in the cold, excruciating pain racked my body, while desperation gripped my soul. My shattered bones and open wounds had left me helpless. Mind drifting, I slipped in and out of consciousness. Hypothermia and frostbite invited death to collect me, but an encouraging voice kept bringing me back.

The voice—*why does he keep talking, why does he want me to stay awake? Hey, Prakash, I just need to shut my eyes for a few minutes. It's so cold, and I'm hurting so much.* Still, my friend's jokes and fanciful stories about tropical beaches distracted me from what promised to be a slow and painful death.

We knew a rescue attempt by foot wouldn't reach me in time. My best chance for survival was a Flight for Life helicopter, but the fierce wind and impending storm pushed this possibility away. Even though Prakash had called for help, we both knew that helicopters and blizzards don't mix. Still, there *had* to be a chance. Eyes frozen shut, I listened for the beating blades—willed them to appear. But there was only the steady hush of the rising wind and Prakash's calm voice.

My broken body lay sprawled across an angled rock, *a frozen tombstone*, I thought. Slipping, slipping, slipping, I balanced on the knife-edge between life and death. As I inched toward a comforting white light behind my closed eyelids, I knew God was offering me a choice: I could give up and die, or I could find the strength to survive and begin a new life. My accident on Mount Rosalie was the defining moment that separated my old life from my existing one. It would change me forever.

# Chapter 1 – Touched By Death

I was cleaning my house and ready for a break, so I grabbed my keys and took off on a shopping adventure. Cruising north on Interstate 25, I headed toward REI, my favorite outdoor gear store. A few yellow leaves, not ready for winter yet, hung on trees on a crisp Saturday afternoon in November, 2010. I knew how they felt. I wasn't ready for winter either and dreaded the cold months ahead. Earlier in the day, I had gone for a long run, and now I needed to buy more cold weather gear for the approaching frozen months.

As I drove, daydreaming about mountains, my ringing phone snapped me back to reality. I reached across the passenger seat and grabbed the phone. An unrecognized number.

"Hello?"

"Hi, Alyson. This is Barry, Chris's friend."

Barry had never called me before. Wary, I replied, "Hi Barry, I know who you are. Chris talks about you all the time. Did he give you my number? Why are you calling me?" In the next instant, my gut took a dive.

Silence. He didn't have to answer.

I exhaled and my next breath was a gasp. I knew. Something horrible had happened to my best friend, my running partner, my mountain climbing partner, my Chris.

Barry croaked, "Alyson, are you sitting down?"

"No, I'm driving. What's wrong? Is Chris okay?"

"Alyson, you need to pull over before I can continue. I don't want you to have an accident."

This was it. Something was wrong. I screamed, "Barry. I'm on the Interstate. I can't pull over." I pleaded, "Tell me what happened. Is Chris okay?"

Finally, Barry answered, but I couldn't make out what he said. I could tell he'd been crying. Barry's voice crackled as he spoke. It was difficult for him to call me with this news.

"Chris was in an ice climbing accident. Alyson, he didn't make it."

A long silence settled over us.

Finally, Barry said, "Alyson? Are you okay?"

In disbelief, I roared, "What the hell do you mean he didn't make it? I was trail running with him the other day."

My lungs lost air and I felt as if someone was pouring cement down my throat. Tears flushed my eyes. My fingers numbed, my foot hit the floor, and I couldn't think about, feel, or understand anything in that moment. Both pain and emotion smashed my heart, eclipsed my soul, and separated me from my body. I realized that I was barreling toward the highway median. I dropped the phone, yanked the wheel right, and with horns blaring at me, narrowly avoided an accident.

After an awkward ending to Barry's call, I pulled into the corner of the REI parking lot and slumped sideways, sobbing.

Christian Pruchnic did risky climbs, but he was one of the most skilled and cautious climbers I knew. He was the chair of the Front Range Section of the American Alpine Club, and he was in the best shape of his life.

Chris had been to my house for a barbecue the weekend before the accident with Josh and my family. While Josh, my husband, sipped a beer, Chris and I had made plans to climb Mount Kilimanjaro and run hundred-mile races. Mount Kilimanjaro was a dormant volcano in Tanzania. At an elevation of 19,341 feet, it was well known for being the fourth most prominent peak in the world and a great destination for mountaineers. Chris was into doing big adventures and traveling far. This type of big adventure was new for me, but I was open and willing to partake in just about anything with Chris; he was so fun to be around and I was hoping to be along for the ride. Chris had talked about running a hundred-mile race in the future. At the time, I didn't fully comprehend what he was talking about: a hundred-mile race? Was he referring to driving a hundred miles? He went on further to describe hundred-mile races. Chris described these as ultra-marathons that were sometimes a hundred miles in length that people did for fun. Ultra-marathons were described as anything over the distance of a full marathon, which is 26.2 miles. At the time, it didn't sound fun; it sounded 100 percent crazy and absurd! Who knew what the future had in store for me. I tried to remain open-minded for just about anything. Chris had the personality of someone who could talk you into just about anything, so from now on, the sky was the limit. He had sparked my interest in long-distance races and at the time, I did not understand how that would change my life.

Now, I could not, would not use the past tense. But reality crept in. Chris was gone. I didn't understand why God took such an amazing person. When we engage in dangerous activities like mountaineering, an accident is always a possibility, and losing Chris made me question my own safety and mortality. Was I next?

As a child, I loved being outside. I adored the freedom of the outdoors, but couldn't anticipate how important it would become for me. As a young adult, I became passionate about hiking and climbing in the mountains. When I stand on the summit of a high peak with the world spread below my feet, only the place and the moment matter. The clean air, brilliant sky, and incredible views push life's struggles to the back burner. While it's wonderful to climb mountains in summer, I found that the high mountains in winter offered challenges, beauty, and isolation from the social world below.

A winter climb can be spectacular with the right conditions. The breathtaking views and serenity found on winter climbs causes my heart to pause and savor the moment. I feel my heart pounding as I survey the world below, and relish the joy of another journey to the top of my world. This was my refuge and my freedom—my salvation.

It's hard to find good winter partners who will get up at 3:00 a.m., drive for hours and then hike up a mountain in freezing temperatures. I often found myself climbing alone in the winter, which was not always the best idea. One time, my sister, Sarah, joined me on a winter hike up Mount Elbert, Colorado's highest peak, and I ran into an old hiking buddy, Prakash Manley, along the trail. Prakash's skill level and speed were like mine, so I knew we could become solid climbing partners.

I first met Prakash through 14ers.com, a website dedicated to Colorado's 14,000-foot peaks. Colorado has 54 mountain peaks exceeding 14,000 feet—known locally as the 14ers—the most in any state. Outdoor enthusiasts visit this website: likeminded individuals looking for information about the 14,000-foot peaks. People you meet on the website have all skill levels but they all have one thing in common, which is a desire to learn more about how to tackle these peaks. The 14ers website became a great resource for me to get information to climb the 14,000-foot mountains in Colorado, and to meet people. In the past, I had done a few group hikes with Prakash and we had enjoyed each other's company. He was fit, fast, and athletic, but more importantly, he was lighthearted and easy-going. He loved hiking in winter—a rare find in a climbing partner—and was always well-prepared.

When you climb any time of the year, it's important to have a partner. Every year Colorado hikers and climbers get lost, caught in avalanches, suffer heart attacks, sprain an ankle or knee, break bones, and develop hypothermia, heat exhaustion, or altitude sickness. A good partner helps mitigate the risk by being there to provide a second opinion on route safety, provide immediate aid in the event of an accident, and if necessary, send for help. A partner can make the difference between life and death during a catastrophic event. I worried about "when," and not "if," because something happens, sooner or later, to anyone who climbs mountains. Meaning, it could be as minor as a small bruise or cut from a tree branch. More serious things can happen such as spraining an ankle, breaking a bone, or getting lost.

## Deer Creek Trailhead - 6:00 a.m.

On Saturday, February 19, 2011, I planned to meet Prakash at the Deer Creek Trailhead at 6:00 a.m. I wanted my husband to hike Rosalie Peak with us, but he declined the invitation.

He said, "You want me to get up at 3:30 in the morning to climb a mountain in sub-zero temperatures on a Saturday?" I left Josh a note with directions to the trailhead, which was an hour away from Denver, in case he changed his mind. I hoped he would come up later and meet me on the descent from the mountain. Otherwise, it was going to be my dog, JB, Prakash, and me.

I didn't feel I was asking much of Josh. What are Saturdays for? We live in Colorado. I knew many people would think what I was asking was crazy. Still, this was Josh, my husband.

A sense of foreboding came over me as I closed the door. It wasn't a premonition of something bad. Climbing had become important to me, but everyone was telling me that I was crazy for chasing mountains, the only real joy in my life. I felt that running and climbing had saved me. I felt joy and peace while running a trail or climbing a peak. I was tired of trying to explain my passions and convince everyone around me that this was important to me. I was tired of feeling guilty about not being like everyone else. I wanted my husband to share these moments with me, but he couldn't do that. I felt miserable, leaving without him, and I was unhappy being alone on most of my outdoor pursuits.

JB and I got into my car. My dog didn't know it, but he kept me from choking on tears. His brown eyes and wagging tail reminded me that he also looked forward to the climb. I was determined to have a wonderful adventure that day and wished I could be free to live life without guilt, condemnation, or excuses. I wanted to live with joy. I decided to stop thinking and focus on enjoying the day's climb.

I arrived at the trailhead a little after 6:00 that morning. Prakash was there, waiting in his Jeep at the lower trailhead to drive us to the upper trailhead. My little Honda Accord couldn't push through the heavy snow blanketing the upper road. With Prakash's 4WD vehicle, we could save two miles of walking on a sixteen-mile hike.

Prakash said, "Hey, get in the car. We'll take every mile we can get; it's winter." JB and I jumped into the Jeep and left my unresolved problems behind. It was good to be with someone who also anticipated a fun day. We couldn't have been happier.

Our plan was to hike 13,575-foot Rosalie Peak in the Mount Evans Wilderness Area and then trek over to one of Rosalie's neighbor peaks if we had time. I had hiked Rosalie a couple of weekends before this trip, since it's close to Denver and has low avalanche danger. Nothing that morning indicated that our climb would be any different than my previous ascent.


## Starting Out - 6:30 a.m.

At the trailhead, we ran into Kevin Baker, another climber who Prakash knew through 14ers.com. Kevin mentioned that he was a member of listsofjohn.com, another mountaineering website.

11

I was already a 14ers.com member and had made many friends through that website, but I had never heard of listsofjohn.com. I was excited to learn more. I wanted to climb new peaks besides Colorado's 54 Fourteeners, and was in a slump because 14ers.com mostly offered information on 14,000-foot peaks. There were many other mountains to climb.

Kevin also planned to climb Mount Rosalie, so he joined our party. Windless blue skies greeted us at the trailhead. The February day looked promising. Using an existing snowshoe trail for the first few miles, we made good time through a pine forest to treeline at 12,000 feet. Kevin and I were using snowshoes and Prakash was using a pair of skis for our Mount Rosalie climb.

When the snowshoe trail ended, I asked Prakash to continue breaking trail above treeline. Once we reached treeline and felt the sun hitting our faces, we stopped to snack, bask in the sunshine, and talk about mountains and meditation. Prakash hovered over a Jetboil stove, cooking ramen noodles. The lightweight stove with its little burner made sense for this tough winter hike.

After our break, we continued to a point where the wind had scoured most of the snow off the rocks, and we cached our snowshoes and skis. At high altitudes, even carrying a little extra weight wears a climber down. The slope above us held little snow, making snowshoes and skis unnecessary. It was a beautiful day. I grinned, watching JB scamper ahead of us. He seemed to know where we were going, but doubled back to make sure.

## Summit - 11:25 a.m.

The day's weather forecast predicted cloudy skies after 11:00 in the morning, with increasing wind and light snow. Bad weather would arrive in the evening, with a strong storm lasting through the next day. Our plan was to reach Rosalie's summit by 11:00 a.m., and then top out on the neighboring peak by noon. The evening forecast called for an 80 percent chance of heavy snow and high winds, but we planned to be back at the trailhead before the bad weather hit. As we neared the top in the late morning, the weather forecast seemed accurate with clouds rapidly moving in. Wind and blowing snow greeted us on Rosalie's frosty 13,575-foot summit at 11:25 a.m. Still fresh in our warm winter gear, we paused to savor the breathtaking view of the world below and around us soaking in the 360-degree views.

Alyson and JB on Rosalie's summit
Photo by Prakash

Prakash, Kevin, and I still felt strong after climbing to Rosalie's summit. We discussed our condition, considered the deteriorating weather, and decided to continue to 13,530-foot "Epaulie," another peak located a little over a mile northwest of Rosalie. The gentle ridge between the two peaks is an easy stroll in summer, but is exposed to high winds in winter. Everything seemed fine to continue, so we started toward "Epaulie."

Descending to the saddle between the peaks, I skidded on wet rock and felt a sharp pain in my left hip. I let out a whimper. Three months prior, I had torn a muscle in my hip flexor running in a 50-kilometer race. Since then, I'd been rehabilitating the injury with physical therapy, and felt that I'd made a huge improvement. I had done many hikes since the injury, and had almost forgotten about it until that moment. My hip burned with pain, but I didn't think I needed help—I just needed to be more careful.

After the slip, the pain in my tender hip slowed my downhill speed. Prakash and Kevin were ahead of me and hadn't seen me fall, nor did they hear my whimper because the stiff wind had snatched it away. I thought about my situation and knew I needed to return to the trailhead, so I sped up my pace to catch up with my partners and tell them about my possible muscle tear. I said they could keep going, but I was turning back. I'd already done Rosalie Peak twice before and figured I'd be fine hiking back alone. Kevin decided to continue on, while Prakash said he'd go back with me. We agreed to meet Kevin near treeline on our descent and finish the rest of the hike together. With my slower speed, we knew he'd easily catch up with us after "Epaulie." Prakash and I turned around and started back toward Rosalie and our descent to treeline, and eventually, the trailhead.

## My Fall - 1:00 p.m.

We climbed back over Mount Rosalie without any problems. On our long descent, we thought that Kevin would catch up with us, but looking back through the swirling snow, he was nowhere in sight. It was too windy to wait on the ridge, so we continued hiking down. The gusty wind had filled in our tracks and we needed Kevin to help beat the trail down, so I could manage with my gimpy leg, but there was no sign of him. It was almost 1:00 in the afternoon when Prakash and I stopped to rest and munch on snacks. Since I was moving slowly, I decided to head down with JB while Prakash finished his apple. He would quickly catch up to me lower down the slope. I was anxious to get off the mountain and to the safety of the trailhead.

Alyson and JB beginning the descent of Rosalie Peak
Photo by Prakash

There was no visible trail above treeline. The terrain, a jumble of rocks, tundra, snow, and ice, wasn't difficult for a healthy mountaineer with two good legs, but in my condition, I figured it was best to pick my way across the shortest, safest route. The slope was steep, but there was no avalanche danger. I decided to take a different route than our ascent line, and join our original route farther downhill to shorten the distance. I anticipated that Prakash would follow my new path, but regardless of which way he went, our paths would intersect in the trees.

I started slowly, stepping over rocks, heading toward treeline. My hip flexor was weak. I turned to see if Prakash was in sight. Not yet, so I continued downhill. Wincing with pain, I babied each step. I knew it was going to be a slow hike back to the car. I approached a 200-foot-long slab of hard snow. I wasn't carrying crampons—a frame of metal spikes lashed to a climber's boots that would have come in handy on this terrain—or other traction devices. I paused at the edge of the hard snow, eying the slope below, and then looked at the long hike around it. Avoiding the snow slope would require

15

many painful steps. I reasoned that if my muscle wasn't torn and I moved carefully, I could safely take the short path across the slope. I stepped down onto the snow and immediately my hip gave out.

Screaming, I skidded face-first down the steep snow, sliding out of control. Down I flew to the bottom of the snow field, where I smashed into a pile of boulders. The crash landing hurt more than my hip injury. I heard and felt my bones snap. Sharp, excruciating pain racked my lower body.

I lay sprawled against the mountainside, head down with arms and legs splayed on the snow. Numbness enveloped me and I clung to my rational mind. *What was broken? My hip? My pelvis? My femur? All three? What am I going to do now?* Too many questions. My brain was overloaded.

I thought, *What if Prakash goes a different way? What if Prakash doesn't find me? I'm dead. Oh, God. What am I going to do? Breathe. Okay, Alyson, gather your wits and assess your injury. You will be okay. You will be able to scoot down on your butt if necessary.* I whispered into the wind, "I'm a survivor." Pain shot through my numbness, and I found new breath for an agonized scream.

I didn't move for ten minutes but it seemed like an eternity. *Where was Prakash?* I felt paralyzed in my tenuous position, attached to the mountain by fear and pain. Time seemed to stop. Then, from out of nowhere, Prakash was beside me. The howling wind muffled his words. He yelled that he heard my screams.

I lay face-down in the snow, shaking in pain. Prakash bent down close to my ear and said, "Hey, what's the matter?"

In a whispery voice threaded with fear, I said, "Prakash, I've got some really bad news. I fell and felt bones breaking in my body. I think my pelvis and leg are broken. I can't move. It hurts. Oh, my God, the pain is killing me."

JB circled around us. He knew I was hurt, but didn't know what to do. My dog whimpered and whined beside me, wanting to help.

As I blurted those words, the reality of our situation hit us both, and our hearts sank. The fierce wind was pushing a severe storm onto the mountain. We both knew it was coming, and that the forecast for that night and the next day called for frigid temperatures, snow, and more wind. Prakash stood in shock, contemplating how he could get me down the 500 vertical feet of mountain to the protected, relative safety of treeline. We knew that if I could make it to the trees, I might be able to survive the night. Trees can make a huge difference in a storm, guarding against the wind and allowing safe passage around trunks and under boughs. For now, I lay exposed to the wind and blowing snow.

"Prakash, cross your fingers for service and let's call for help." My hiking partner fished inside my backpack and grabbed the GPS and phone. He turned them on, and we waited. *Please let there be a signal.*

"Hallelujah! You have phone service—and a full battery!"

I needed Search and Rescue, hopefully Flight for Life, fast. I didn't know who to call first, so I rang my husband, but it went to voicemail. My heart sank. *Where was he?* Next, I called Shawn, a hiking friend. He answered.

I described our position through tears and pain. Shawn calmly handled the news and coached Prakash on using my GPS to give the coordinates for our location to Search and Rescue. Prakash rattled off coordinate numbers, described the changing weather, our emergency gear, how long he thought we could last, and our immediate plans. Shawn agreed to our plan of action and said he would call the Park County Sheriff's Department. Another person now had our position, which was vital.

A few minutes later, we received a call from Sarah at the Park County Sheriff's office. Her voice was similar to my little sister, Sarah's. I thought about my sister and was glad she wasn't with me in this mess. If she were here, I'd be more worried about her freaking out than about saving myself. This other Sarah, the one at the sheriff's office, asked about our position and my injuries.

Prakash explained that I had no visible external bleeding, but probably broke a femur and possibly my pelvis, and that I was immobile. Sarah expressed concern that I likely had significant internal bleeding. She told Prakash to only call 911 while we were out there, and that a Flight for Life helicopter from Saint Anthony's Hospital in Denver had been dispatched. Sarah said the chopper could only evacuate me, leaving my partner and dog to descend alone. We were fine with that. Prakash was prepared for the weather, and my dog would go with him.

I was lucky to have Prakash there. He was always optimistic. Prakash was a true hero, my hero. JB, my dog, wanted to stay by my side. I saw it in his eyes, but I knew he would be fine descending with Prakash.

Questions popped into my mind. *Could Flight for Life even find me?* Of course, they could. They had our coordinates. They could fly right to us. *Would they be able to move me to the chopper?* Knowing the severity of my injuries, they'd have a rigid stretcher or litter to transport me to the helicopter, or they could carry me by hand. Prakash could help too. The whole evacuation would only take a few minutes. The transfer would be painful, but I had to get into the chopper. *Would they have pain medication?* The chopper was coming from a hospital; surely, they would have pain meds.

I lay sprawled across the icy slope, anchored only by the weight of my pack and the traction of my boot on a rock. Prakash knew I needed to be on a more stable, flat spot. The angle of the slope was steep; one wrong move could send my careening down the mountain. Moving to a flatter location for a possibly long stay was going to be essential for my survival. Prakash helped move me. The best way to tolerate pain was putting my feet close together. Prakash held my feet as I turned and maneuvered into a sitting position. We were sure that my left femur was broken and possibly my pelvis. He helped me slide onto a protruding rock slab. I was still sitting on snow, and we knew it would eventually soak through my pants, leading to hypothermia. Hypothermia—a dangerous drop in body temperature—could be my demise. The condition is usually caused by prolonged exposure in cold temperatures. I was in this very predicament and wasn't sure how to escape it.

Prakash was ahead of me. "Alyson, will you let me put my ski skins under you? You'll get cold sitting directly on the snow."

He was asking me to endure pain once more, but I said, "Okay."

Ski skins provide skis with traction and are used on the bottom of skis to hike uphill, and then removed to descend. The material was thick and longer than my legs, so this seemed like a good idea. Prakash pulled the skins beneath me, and the new pain made me scream.

Prakash scanned the slope above for any sign of Kevin and a better place to move me for a helicopter evacuation, but there was no sign of our friend and no better place for me to lie. The pain from my slightest movements convinced me that I wasn't going to crawl or scoot across the slope. I needed outside help. I needed a helicopter.

When I could breathe again, I said, "Prakash, will you stay with me through this? If I die on this mountain, I don't want to be alone."

Without hesitation, he answered, "Yeah, I'll stay. I'll watch for Kevin and send him down for help. He can take JB with him and I'll stay until help comes."

His answer soothed me. It gave me strength and a stronger will to survive. This was a thought that returned to me over and over in the hours to come. *Thank you, Prakash. I don't want to face death alone.* I knew my situation wasn't good. I asked myself how I was going to get off this mountain alive. I'm a realist and knew I was in serious trouble. While I didn't know the extent of my injuries, I knew that a fast rescue was improbable. I couldn't move and I was bleeding internally. If bleeding to death didn't finish me off, hypothermia would.

Prakash reassured me that he wouldn't leave. His words gave me a slender thread of hope. Unable to move, I felt the cold quickly setting, chilling me to the bone. Prakash was risking his own life to save me; how could I not give everything I had to stay alive?

I gripped my phone in my hand, waiting for a call from Search and Rescue or Flight for Life. It rang, but the display told me it was my husband, Josh. I wanted to answer but whatever was left in the battery was crucial for my rescue. Minutes later, my phone rang again: my mom, then my brother Daniel.

I desperately wanted to answer the calls. I wanted to tell my mom how much I loved her and the rest of my family. It might be the only chance I'd have to hear her voice again. Prakash reminded me to not answer the phone. He said I wasn't going to die on this mountain, and would have other opportunities to tell them I loved them.

The calls stopped and silence settled in. I stared at the black emptiness on my phone's screen, thinking, *What did I get myself into? How did this happen? I've just started to live, and now I'm going to die.*

# Chapter 2 – Flight For Life

We finally got a call from the sheriff's office asking about my symptoms, injuries, the weather, and other details. They asked if there was room for the Flight for Life chopper to land. Prakash had already spotted a flat spot about 150 feet from us and told them yes. Our spirits soared at the thought of a rescue.

In the meantime, my black lab kept trying to get close to me. He stepped on my feet trying to cuddle with me, causing shockwaves of pain. It crushed my heart to yell at him to get away. My poor pup, JB, wanted to get warm and keep me warm; he wanted to protect his "mommy."

Prakash scanned the ridges and mountain above looking for Kevin. We still hoped to send JB down with him but without our GPS coordinates, finding us would be nearly impossible. We knew that Kevin didn't even know I was in trouble. We hoped the worst weather would be delayed so both Kevin and Flight for Life could have better visibility. Worst case, Kevin would hear the chopper and hopefully know that something was wrong.

## New Hope - 2:30 p.m.

Around 2:30 in the afternoon we heard the chopper. The sound of the beating blades sent my spirit sky high, and I surged with relief. *I was going to make it.* I would be in a hospital bed before dinner. *Oh, thank God.*

We spotted the chopper flying over the wrong area. *How could that be? They had our coordinates.* Clouds swirled, signaling the approaching storm, and precious minutes ticked away. Uncertain fear foiled my sky-high mood. Prakash faced the chopper sound, took off his brightly-colored shell jacket, and waved it wildly. I was on the phone with the sheriff's office trying to guide the pilot to our exact location. More precious minutes escaped. Still on the phone, I gave them new directions and told them to look for the waving jacket. They finally spotted us.

The chopper touched down in a swirl of snow, as the impending snowstorm still threatened to close our escape route. Time was running out. The rescuers would have to pick me up and carry me to the helicopter. I braced for the pain, knowing that was going to hurt like hell, but that once I was on the chopper, I'd get medication.

After the snow settled, we saw four people on board: a pilot, co-pilot, and two nurses. The nurses, a man and a woman, jumped off and ran toward us. They wore white hospital uniforms with name tags, short-sleeved shirts, street shoes, and shorts. They weren't dressed for the cold or prepared for a mountain rescue. Halfway to us, they stopped.

Despite our detailed phone communication, the chopper crew was unaware of my severe injuries. We had said that I had a broken femur and a possible broken pelvis. We hadn't asked for any particular treatment, but every medical professional knows that these severe injuries render a victim unable to walk or even hobble. It didn't look like they had a litter.

The pilot yelled above the wind, "Get in the chopper. Quick! We've got three minutes before the weather hits."

Prakash couldn't believe they had flown up there in shorts and with no equipment. He shouted, "We can't move her. She needs to be stabilized. I think she may have a broken pelvis."

As the nurses ran back toward the chopper, I pushed up from the slab, and hollered, "Can you leave me some pain medication? Anything?" For a fleeting instant, I was convinced they must be going back to the chopper for meds and a sleeping bag.

The pilot sat at the controls with the blades humming at speed. Without looking at me, he glanced at the co-pilot and the clouds, and waved the nurses back to the chopper. They hopped in and slammed the door shut. Blades revved, digging into the air and kicking up a mushroom cloud of snow.

The chopper took off. Whoosh. They left us with nothing. I watched it leave without me, turn toward Denver, and disappear into the clouds. I listened to the receding whop, whop, whop, and then pondered the silence. A blast of wind hit me. I released my grip, sagged back to the slab, and went into shock. Suddenly, I couldn't breathe and thought I was dying. Panic rose, paralyzing my thoughts.

I shut my eyes, lay still, and forced myself to breathe the panic out. When the coldness of the slab made me ache, I focused on that discomfort. Slowly, my thoughts settled. *How could they abandon me here with nothing? No sleeping bag, no tent, no drugs, nothing.* I couldn't understand why the chopper crew was so unprepared for my injuries and the obvious winter conditions. It made no sense. Flight for Life was my best chance, and the sound of silence stole what was left of my strength. Exhaling, I was defeated and deflated. I thought about the cold and all the blood leaking out of me internally and whimpered, "I'm done. I'm toast." I closed my eyes and endured what seemed like an eternity of silence.

When I opened my eyes, I expected Prakash to cheer me up with his usual, positive spin, but his back was turned to me. *What was he thinking?* I figured he was trying to collect himself and didn't want me to see any sign of weakness.

Finally, he turned and said, "I guess I don't blame them for leaving, Alyson. The storm clouds were 50 feet above us, moving at 50 miles per hour, and looked like a cluster of bombers trying to break formation and pass each other."

Ah, there was the positive Prakash I knew. I blurted, "They could have tossed a sleeping bag out the door. If they had read their GPS, there would have been enough time to get me to the chopper."

Prakash was already thinking about Plan B, but my heart continued to sink. The shouting, confusion, and ludicrous ending to the anxiously awaited rescue had drained me both physically and emotionally. Any thin hopes for survival had taken flight with the chopper. Clever conversation couldn't help me now. I had no energy left to grieve. Each shallow breath made me ache as I faced the realization of a frigid, lingering death. Soon, fear was all I had and I closed my eyes, wishing for a quick end to my misery.

# Chapter 3 – Dark Memories

I pried my eyelids free from frost, fully expecting to see the Pearly Gates, Saint Peter, or some sign from above. Instead, I saw wind sweeping across the mountain. Falling snow bit my face. Maybe I hadn't always been the best person, but I had a good heart and would never do anything intentionally to hurt anyone. *I should be in Heaven by now.* Blinking the driving snow from my eyes, I realized I was still alive. I wasn't dead yet.

I was still alive, trapped above treeline with a broken body during a growing winter storm. I raised my hand in pain and brushed the snow from my face, exposing my hand and arm to bitter cold. I slowly curled my face away from the wind and tucked my arm against my side. I knew I was still broken and bleeding, but was too cold to think about any of it.

A flood of memories raced into my mind. They pushed me to a secret place I had been avoiding. I wasn't sure if this was my life flashing before me as I died, or if it was a last-ditch attempt to make sense of what had never made sense, a last chance to reconcile the conflicts in my life and finally heal old wounds; a chance to forgive and be forgiven. I closed my eyes and followed a flow of memories. The cruel cold reminded me of another night many years before.

"Mom, why is dad doing this? It's a school night. I want to go to bed. Mom, I'm freezing. Why can't we go inside? Mom, it's snowing. It's January and the heater in our car doesn't work. Mom, I'm scared."

I was in the third grade at Dartmouth Elementary School in Aurora, Colorado, too young to understand that my father was an alcoholic, or comprehend what our family would endure for the next ten years. I couldn't understand what caused my dad to abuse my mother, my three brothers, my sister, and me. As usual, my father was drunk when he came home from work that night. He launched into a screaming fight with my mother. This escalated until my mom couldn't handle it anymore, so she and I escaped to a local bar. At the time, I didn't know why we left my brothers and sister with Dad, but it brought his anger to a frightening new level.

I was the only one in the family who ever stood up to my dad. I said it how it was, called it as I saw it, and always spoke what I thought was the blunt truth. In these situations, the truth hurts, and I believe that drove him nuts. Dad always needed to be right and always have the last word. I never sat still for that, so he treated me the worst. Mom probably took me to the bar and not my brothers and sister because she thought I could trigger my dad's big bomb of a temper that was waiting to blow.

Throughout my childhood, both my parents were heavy drinkers. My father drank because of work stress and having five children to support. Mom drank to numb her raw emotions and to deal with my father. They used alcohol to escape from their unhappiness.

At the bar that evening, my mom had a few drinks and tried to relax. I had my favorite pizza and played a game of shuffleboard. It felt good to be out of the house, away from the fighting and screaming. After a few hours, my mom decided it was time to go home and face things. She hoped dad would have cooled down, but we soon found out what waited for us. As we pulled into our quiet, dark cul-de-sac, a cold shiver ran down my back. It didn't feel right. "Now what?" I thought.

Our ranch-style home was dark, the blinds shut, and the doors closed. Okay, it was winter, and maybe dad was trying to conserve heat. I often heard him complain about the heating bill. But with our big family, a light was always on somewhere in the house.

We pulled into the driveway and I saw two pillows and two blankets sitting on the front porch, covered in snow. My mom saw them, too. She tried to remain calm for my sake, but I knew she was mortified. We were both thinking the same thing and didn't have to speak to know what the other felt.

I looked up to my mom. I loved her and often felt her torture. I knew other families whose parents had divorced, and I always wondered why she didn't leave my dad. I knew she believed she was doing the right thing for us kids. God love her for that.

I looked into her face, red with cold and humiliation. I can still see the hurt and bewildered look on her face. She didn't understand how dad could be so cruel. I blinked back tears and tried not to look into her swollen blue eyes. I closed my eyes and imagined our warm living room behind the locked front door. I could see the busy kitchen behind it and the hallway to the bedrooms on the left with kids running back and forth. I could see the ceramic figurines mom had made and painted for our home.

*Oh mom. I can't look at you. I hurt for you.* I could see my bedroom with my warm bed and soft pillow inviting me to sleep. I couldn't see how we were going to ever get back inside or if this nightmare would ever end.

I finally opened my eyes and looked at Mom. She was not a big woman, but that night she seemed so small, frail, and afraid. My heart was breaking. I felt sorry for her and angry with dad. I was overcome with strong emotions that were hard for a child to handle. I just wanted it to go away.

Mom fumbled for her keys and started up the sidewalk. I followed her. She tried to stick her key into the lock, and then discovered that dad had broken a key in it.

"Okay mom, what's going on? Why is dad doing this?" She grabbed her garage door opener and pressed the button, but nothing happened. He must have unplugged that too.

"What's wrong with him? Why is he doing this? I just don't understand."

I didn't know what to feel. This was my father. How could he treat his daughter and wife this way? *He's supposed to love us.* I was numb from the cold and an overwhelming sadness and anger. I looked at my small hands and saw that they were blue and shaking. I was afraid, too.

We went to the rear of the house. I climbed over a fence, opened the gate, and let my mom into the backyard. I scanned the neighbors' houses hoping no one could see us. We knocked on the back door and pleaded with dad to let us in. We got no response, but we did hear my sister and brother crying for him to let us in. We moved over to my older brother Jason's room and banged on his window. It was late, cold, snowing, and a school night. Jason tried, but dad wouldn't let him open the door. We heard him yell at Jason for considering it. Was it time for more screaming, or should we break a window? No, that would only enrage him.

Crying, I said, "What is wrong with dad? I know he's drunk, but does he really think we are going to sleep outside or in the car in a winter storm in the middle of January? I have school tomorrow." I asked my mom if I could go to my best friend Laura's house and sleep there. She said it was too late, and she needed me with her. I knew that I needed to look out for her and my little brothers and sister. They needed me as much as I needed them. I was nine years old going on thirty.

After knocking on windows for 30 minutes, we were too cold to continue. Our hands and bodies were spastic from the cold. My mom held me for warmth and we cried in each other's arms. We finally gave up trying to get into the house and went back to the car. My mom turned on the engine, but the heater was broken. We sat there shivering for a few hours. I finally fell asleep, hoping to wake from this bad dream. Somewhere between 2:00 and 3:00 a.m., my mom woke me up. The garage door was open, and it looked like my dad was letting us into the house. *But to what?*

I raced to my bedroom, crawled beneath my covers, and lay there shivering. The evening's events were bewildering. As I began to doze, the yelling started again. I didn't care anymore. I didn't want the responsibility of taking care of my mom or my brothers and sister. I just wanted to be warm. I dug my head deep under the pillow to block the screaming and went to sleep.

Why wouldn't my dad let us in that night? How could he deliberately leave us outside to freeze? Did he know what it was like for a child to be cold and terrified? Why wouldn't he let us in? Did he feel regret or sadness when he sobered up and remembered what he had done? Did he even remember? Why did he take out his frustrations on us? Why? Why would he try to hurt those he was supposed to love and care for? Why? I really don't care why, but if I really don't care, why does it still bother me? Why can't I put this to rest? Am I going to be haunted for the rest of my life by memories I can't change or understand?

I don't know how to change them. I can't spend my life grieving. Somehow, I have to come to terms with my dad. Trying to shake the memory from my mind, my head involuntarily rolled to one side.

Little Alyson

Ow! This new pain roused me on my freezing night on the mountain. What would I give to have a pillow right now, even one covered with snow? I couldn't hear my parents screaming anymore. I was the one screaming now. The place where my head rested on the ground was numb with cold. I rolled my head to spread the misery.

When reality came into focus, I noticed Prakash rummaging in his pack to find his emergency, super-warm, 800-fill down jacket. He wrapped it around my feet, which were slowly succumbing to the cold. Prakash came up with an emergency hand warmer set, and stuffed one into each of my mittens. Then, he put his Everest expedition mitten shells over my mittens. Next, he produced an emergency painkiller and lifted a Nalgene bottle of water to my mouth so I could swallow the pill. My hands were planted firmly on the slab to take pressure off my leg, and I couldn't think about moving them to give myself a drink.

Prakash said, "I hope this pill is better than nothing, Alyson. Do you want any tea? Ramen? Food? Water? You don't have to drink my crappy Gatorade. I have real water."

"No, I'm good."

He gave me most of his extra clothing, taking better care of me than the hospital nurses who abandoned me. The gesture was profound, but I couldn't express gratitude in my compromised state of mind.

My movements brought pain, and I lay back again to breathe it out. I stared into a sheet of falling snow, and then rolled my head away from the cold, white blanket. Even with demons running free, I was safer inside my head.

## Jason

I was always independent, but our large family didn't give me much alone time. I had an older brother, Jason, two younger brothers, Daniel and Kyle, and a younger sister, Sarah. Everyone had a role and place in our family.

Jason would always beat up on me. We were close in our younger years, but later, we grew apart. Jason played basketball and was about my height. Of course, being a guy, he was heavier and more muscular. Approaching adulthood, Jason and I did not get along.

He married Jonni when he was 19, and they had their first of four children. Jason grew up faster than most kids. He had become a somber man, much too old for his years. He lost the spark that should have been in his eyes. He loved his children very much, but he was serious about everything. I wondered if Jonni had done something to him to take the joy from his life. Sadly, Jonni and I hated each other. I hated her for taking my brother and for the way she treated him. I think she hated me because I was free from the responsibilities that they struggled with.

As children, Jason gave me a hard time for wanting freedom and not kids. I never understood why everyone should have kids. I asked myself if not wanting my own children made me a bad person or if, on the other hand, I a better person for realizing it.

I grew up watching my mom sacrifice herself for us kids. I saw how Jason's children changed the course of his life. I didn't want to be controlled by other people or forfeit my dreams by having children. I needed freedom to achieve my goals, and I longed for a life spent embracing my passions. My goals were different from Jason's, and I learned that that was all right.

I missed my brother Jason and wondered why he shunned me. Would he ever be my big brother again? I wished our relationship was different. I often thought the wedge between us was instigated by Jonni. It appeared to me that she seemed to control his thoughts and movements. What was the hold that she had on him? Was she jealous of the closeness I once had with Jason? Why couldn't she see that alienating him from our family hurt him and us?

As I lay against the cold rock, I understood that I needed to survive so I could mend the fence between Jason and myself. I wanted my big brother back. I needed to explain to him that my life choices were mine alone. Perhaps, I might accomplish things that gave others the courage to follow their own dreams. Perhaps I could help others understand that they could survive horrible events, that they deserved happiness. Maybe I could help Jason be free to be himself. I wished he knew how much I loved him. I wanted him to be happy. I wanted my brother back. I had to see him again. *I hoped more than anything that Jason could get a second opportunity at life, and one day find true happiness.*

I am finally free of the chains of my horrific childhood and the lack of self-esteem brought on by years of abuse. I am no longer willing to be controlled by others or by addictions. Jason, you should understand that. We share many painful experiences, I want to share joy. We deserve to be happy.

I couldn't think about Jason anymore as I lay on the cold slab. I sobbed for Jason and for myself. If I die here, I thought, I know Prakash will tell Jason that I loved him.

## Daniel

My brother Daniel was the middle child. We were always close. We played together and got along except for a few modest fights. I played adventure games with Daniel that put us in a different world. We would be movie stars or famous athletes in a distant land. If we imagined it, we played it, and we helped each other get through childhood.

As we grew older, we got into trouble together. I regret getting Daniel to smoke marijuana and drink liquor. We went snowboarding often, smoked too much pot, and made some bad decisions. Sometimes, Daniel and I ditched class so we could party and drink together. After that drinking and drug stage, I discovered a passion for climbing mountains, and we enjoyed several special climbs. These experiences brought us closer.

Daniel matured into one of the finest men I know. He found an amazing woman named Meggie, and they were excited about marriage and children. *What would this do to my relationship with Daniel?* I was happy for them, but fearful of the inevitable changes. Meggie is a blonde spitfire who knows where she wants to go and how to get there. Daniel is kind-hearted and devilishly handsome. Meggie and Daniel are good together. I like her, and I think she likes me. She loves and supports our mother. But I am afraid that Daniel will change like Jason. Surely Meggie would not want him to turn away from his family. Family is important to Meggie. They will be good parents, because they're both nurturing.

I thought about how much I loved Daniel. I worried about dying on the mountain and not being able to say goodbye to him. I wanted him to know how proud I was to be his sister and proud of all he had done. I wanted to tell him to always love and respect Meggie, and to love and cherish their children. I wanted him to remember me with a smile. *I have to survive this. I refuse to say good-bye. I wanted to see Daniel and Meggie's children. I wanted to be part of their lives.*

## Sarah

I was intensely close with my sister, Sarah. She was involved with the family pets and usually did her own thing, but eventually Sarah ran marathons and climbed mountains with me. We were different, but when we were together, we had loads of fun. Most of the family thought she was weird, but she became one of my best friends and favorite hiking partners.

Sarah is kind and beautiful, with blonde hair, blue eyes, and a robust athletic figure. She freely shares a beautiful smile with friends, family, and strangers. I always enjoyed Sarah's easy-going attitude and her ability to enjoy varied activities. She balances life better than me, and I'm jealous of her for that.

I've usually had one interest at the expense of everything else. Climbing and running are my obsessions, but for Sarah they're just enjoyable activities. Sarah does crazy things with me, but our similarities often cause us to butt heads. Our athletic philosophy is quite different. I train hard and stay in shape by running and hiking up small peaks close to home every day and I carefully watch my diet.

Sarah doesn't like to train, eats poorly, and shows up for athletic "sufferfests" to endure the pain. She is amazing, since no matter how little she has trained, she succeeds through sheer determination. She mostly enjoys the experience, even if she pays for it later. Sarah's feet seem to love blisters. Maybe one day she will take my advice and buy proper shoes.

*If I die on the mountain, it would destroy Sarah. Therefore, I can't die. We have too much left to do together. She needs me.* I regret not being there for her and not spending more time with her. I wish she knew how glad I am to have her as a sister, how proud I am of the strong independent woman she has become. I needed to tell her those things and support her in her life choices.


## Kyle

Kyle, my youngest brother, was always the 'rat' of us five siblings. He told mom or dad about anything we did wrong. Frankly, we didn't like him until he grew out of his tattletale stage. I felt bad, since Kyle was the youngest child and endured the most mental abuse. While it wasn't always directed at him, he was constantly surrounded by it. I know this messed him up.

I care about Kyle because he has a big heart for other people. His joyful personality is contagious. He's a person you want to be around. He seems to not have a care in the world, but I know that serious pain hides behind his cheerful face. I know that the conflicts of our life sometimes overwhelm him. He is a kind and gentle soul who has buried his pain somewhere deep inside. Every once in a while, the pain surfaces and Kyle has a panic attack. *I could help him so much. I can't die now because Kyle needs me. My baby brother needs his big sister.*

## Mom

There wasn't much for me to measure up to as I grew up. My parents didn't pressure me to do amazing things or excel in school and life. It was acceptable to be mediocre or less. My mom's stay-at-home job was raising her five children. I remember her yelling and screaming at us and fighting with my dad. The incessant screeching and hollering created an unhealthy and unstable atmosphere. It was mom shrieking at us, dad roaring at us, or their rage directed at each other. It was a horrible environment for children and a terrible example of how to live life.

Some early memories are of days when my mom ran an in-home day care. Our house was filled with children who created a constant chaos. Kids running amok meant that we never got much individual attention. How could my mom raise her own children when she tended six or eight others? We kept ourselves entertained. We were able to make it work in our younger years, but eventually, we got into trouble.

Despite my memories of mom yelling at me, I loved her. We were unified by our distaste for my father. *Our relationship wobbled through the years, but now,* I thought as I lay on the rock, *that was no reason to die.*

My mom had become one of my best friends. If I could only apologize for all the mean things I said to her and all the times I treated her badly. *I'm sorry, mom. I love you. I want you to be happy and safe.* She deserves that much. After years of being berated and beaten down, she doesn't know her strength or capabilities. She needs to know she is loved. I want to be there to help her.

# Dad

My dad owned a car detail business that provided for my family and kept a roof over our heads. Most of my childhood memories of my dad are miserable. He is my tormentor. Most memories involve drinking, yelling, fighting, or screaming. I dreaded that my dad would show up at one of my sporting events.

When I played competitive soccer and volleyball, he was a huge embarrassment. He was usually drunk, so I denied that he was my father. I never heard anything positive come out of his mouth. He yelled at me to do better, or bellowed that I wasn't doing something well enough. He also hollered at other girls on the team. His bad behavior continued for years and spread to my brothers' and sister's events.

As I grew up, my feelings for my dad and his treatment of us became stronger and hard to suppress. *If I die now on this slab,* I thought, *I imagine my father showing up at my memorial saying, "I told you so. If only she had listened to me." Good grief. I can't die. He can't be right.* He's my father and I do care about him and love him, and I still want his approval. I have to sort my mess of feelings about him out. I need to come to terms with him so I can be free of the pain he's caused. *I'm sorry for whatever made him act the way he did, but I have to save myself. I can't ignore it any longer.*

Prakash called the Park County Search and Rescue again. "Hey Sarah, the chopper left without Alyson."

"Yeah, sorry about that," Sarah said. "They missed the weather window for the pickup. We'll get ground teams out to you guys."

"Okay. How long?"

"At least four hours."

Four hours meant it would be eight o'clock before they contacted us. We needed to dig in and work on staying fired up, motivated, and positive about the outcome.

I said to Prakash, "Ask them for morphine."

"Yo, send us some morphine?"

"We can't do that, but I'm sure the rescue teams will be able to handle the situation. Oh, don't feed her anything or give her anything to drink since she needs to be ready for general anesthesia at the hospital."

"But she'll get hypothermic faster without food or drink."

"Good point. Okay, but please keep it to a minimum and only when necessary."


## The Athletic Child

I always played sports and had a physique suitable for many activities. I played baseball, kickball, hide-n-seek, and had snowball fights in the cul-de-sac with my brothers, sister, and neighborhood friends. It was a childhood blast. In school, I started with gymnastics, but soon became too tall for spinning. I played soccer for about ten years but, with my height, thought that volleyball would be good to try. I did more than try. I played volleyball on a competitive team called Front Range. I also played soccer and volleyball for my school teams.

Team sports were my only escape from household dramas, putting me into a safe arena. I made friends, enjoyed supportive coaches, and felt like part of a family. I watched how other parents treated their children, and I knew that my home life was badly messed-up.


## Church

My mom bribed us to pay attention during Mass. "Okay, whoever can tell me what the priest talked about during the sermon will get five dollars." We went to church every week for the first 18 years of my life. I hated it. There were a few times I missed Mass in those years, but only because of extreme circumstances.

Church never made sense to me. The priest talked about doing the right things in life, while my parents did the exact opposite. Seeing hypocrisy in action left me not wanting to attend church and failed to convince me that it had good long-term effects.

I hated it because it was forced on me. My mom wanted us to grow up the way she did, with church being a major part of life. She even went to a Catholic school. I went to Sunday school every week, and then had my first communion. I did the same for reconciliation and also went to confirmation classes. I sang in the church choir and did volunteer work with my friend Laura during the holidays. Laura's mom worked at the church, and it was my home away from home. It was a safe place to be, but only because my home life was ridiculous.

Many church people I met were nice, and projected positive thoughts, which stood in sharp contrast to my life. I never gained anything substantial from my church time or going through the motions to make my mom happy. Church was just an escape from home, but it did lay a foundation for me to later fly.

Alyson preparing to fly

36

Over the years I've gained a new view on religion, God, and what works for me. Everyone should choose to do what they feel is natural and right. Religion is different for each person, and one's beliefs should not be forced upon another. I found an opposite view of religion that was better for me, where others can have different beliefs and views about God. I accept each person for who they are and not what I want them to be. Now my church is mountaintops where I feel the presence of my Creator and view his spectacular work.

## Laura

Laura was my best friend. We met in preschool and grew up together. We went to elementary, middle, and high school. She lived down the street, we played sports together, and our families were close. Our dads were drinking buddies. However, Laura's family was more stable than mine, so I spent much of my time at her home. Our birthdays were one day apart, so we had big two-day celebrations every year.

I still cherish our friendship and fondly remember the time I spent with her family. I was sad that we moved apart as we grew older, but that was my fault. Laura stuck with the good kids, while I went in a different direction. If I could tell Laura I'm sorry, I would.

Laura and Alyson

I rarely had sleepovers at my house because I was afraid my drunken dad would do horrendous things around my friends. I didn't want people to know about my home life. Sometimes Laura or other girlfriends spent the night, but it was carefully planned. Once when I was in sixth grade, Laura and Alana spent the night. We watched a movie upstairs on the hide-a-bed. The TV was loud, but we could hear a banging noise in the background. I pretended that my dad was hammering nails, putting pictures on the wall. My friends bought it at first, but after hours of the same noise, I sagged. Already embarrassed, I went to my dad's bedroom to see what was going on. He lay on his bed with a wooden bat repeatedly pounding the wall. I asked what he was doing and if he would please stop. He started yelling and I began crying. I pleaded with him to stop because my friends were over and it was embarrassing. He refused to stop.

As hard as it was to have girlfriends during my childhood, having a boyfriend was even worse. I never invited a guy into the house because of my dad's bad behavior. When he found out I was dating a black dude, I thought he would kill me. Freedom of choice? Oh no, not in my house.

Peer pressure, boys, and destructive behavior dominated my life during middle school. I met the wrong crowd and started a tug of war between hanging out with the right or wrong people. I had my sports and teammates that I considered good friends, but then there was the troublesome group that drank, smoked, and ditched class. I wavered between the two groups. From what I watched growing up, smoking and drinking seemed normal so I was drawn to the bad crowd. It seemed easier to escape with them than through my sports. When I got older, the problems at home worsened, so sports were not enough. I needed more to escape. I needed to numb the emotional pain I carried with me every day.

I was always a mediocre student, and my grades were about average. I never fully applied myself in school, and only did enough to pass. My focus flitted from subject to subject, and my attention span was short. I constantly worried about the next battle at home and dreamed about a better life. Since I didn't see a route to that better life, I wasn't concerned about excelling in school. My parents never pushed me toward excellence, so why should I push myself? Average was acceptable at home, so that's how I went through life.

*A better life?* I asked. *First, I have to get off this mountain alive.* My palms were still pressed down on the slab to take pressure off my leg, but now my hands and forearms felt numb. Carefully, I raised one mitten-clad hand, then the other. A bit of good news was that the cold had slightly numbed the pain in my broken leg. I heard Prakash stomping behind me.

Every bad episode from my childhood made me the person that I am today, and those events inspired me to seek something better. I needed to believe in myself, and to look harder at my life's possibilities. Now, in my home life, I need relations that are more serene, kinder, and peaceful. For my passion, I know there is some kind of performance that I can find for myself that I have always dreamed about. I have found serenity and peace on every mountain I climb. I refuse to settle for a mediocre life. I'm better than that, and I can achieve more whether my family believes in me or not. I have to let some people go, family or not. There is only so much negativity that I can take from another person before that person needs to be cut out of my life. I want to help others that may be stuck in the same cycle of abuse. We cannot allow ourselves to be conquered by fear and feelings of inadequacy. We are each worthwhile. We each have a purpose; we just have to find it, act upon it, and believe in it.

*Please God, if you can hear me, let me make it, and allow me to make a difference in this world. Help me find someone who will accept me for who I am and love me without reservation. I need to be loved. Please give me the strength to survive this test. Please help me.*

I wondered how many times we have all promised to be good or change our ways if God would just help us out of this one bad situation. But this was not a kid who had broken a window or teenager who had dented the family car. This was life or death. This was my life or death. The stakes were as high as they could be, and I wasn't in much of a bargaining position. I was too young to die. I never really had a chance to live my life. Feeling sorry for myself wasn't a wonderfully positive thing, but it helped me to see what I had to change in my life if I survived. My childhood was a nightmare, but I was an adult now. I could make my own choices and act upon them without guilt or regret. My path was becoming clearer. Could there be a little ray of light leading me out of this bleak darkness which was now consuming my soul and stealing my breath?

# Chapter 4 – Nightmare

When Ashley's mom dropped me off, I said, "I'm so hungry. I hope Mom made spaghetti for dinner tonight. Hey, thanks for the ride, Ashley. See you tomorrow at school and volleyball practice." I was in eighth grade.

The Athletic Adolescent

I grabbed my gym bag, shut the car door, and walked toward the house. I was finally home from school after a three-hour volleyball practice and was starving. It was midweek, around 6:00 p.m. I wanted to relax, eat, do homework, and watch TV.

This incident haunted me for years. I have nightmares about that night and sometimes it seems like it happened yesterday. I usually wake up in a panic and cold sweat. That was the night that I believed my dad was going to kill my mom in front of us kids.

Sometimes I ask why I'm messed up in my head, why I have addictive behaviors, and why I've sometimes had different personalities. In the past, I considered these issues to be my parents' fault and I blamed them for my problems. I know now that I have to take responsibility for what I do and how I act. I know that the examples our parents set for us play a vital role in our behaviors and can have a detrimental effect on us. I've never understood why people have children when they don't want them or aren't capable of nurturing them. Many people have children for the wrong reasons.

On that night, I walked to the front door and heard screaming. I looked back to see if Ashley and her mom had driven away yet. The last thing I wanted was for them to hear the screaming. I thought, "Great, mom and dad are at it again. This is perfect. There goes my relaxing evening, again."

My dad is often irrational about many things, but when it involves politics, watch out. When you flip the political switch in my father's head, rational conversation ends. This night was in November 1992 during the presidential election between George H. W. Bush and Bill Clinton.

If anyone in the house spoke a word about liking a Democrat, he or she needed to pack a bag and find a new place to live. I remember a few times when I said something positive about a certain Democrat, and my dad went nuclear. I couldn't dare say that I would vote for a Democrat. I thought every person had the right to make their own decision about their vote, but that was never the story at our home, and still isn't, even to this day.

It was obvious that he was intoxicated. I knew the routine when my parents began fighting and how it would spiral out of control. I would try to protect my younger brothers and sister. My oldest brother Jason usually played referee to make sure things didn't get out of control, although they often did. Jason always looked out for my mom.

My dad was incensed that Bill Clinton won the election so he attacked mom for no reason. She stood there catching his wrath, then broke down and said something back to him. He flew into a roaring rage and charged at her. We were in the kitchen, and mom darted for the hallway. Dad followed, lunged, and grabbed her. He landed on top of her and started choking her. My brothers and sister were screaming. I was crying. I thought he was going to kill her at that moment.

I yelled, "Oh my God, he's strangling her. Jason! Jason, get him off of her. He's going to kill her!"

Jason scrambled toward my parents, grabbed at dad, heaved with a surprising strength, and managed to get him off mother. She lay on the floor gasping, and then started crawling down the hallway towards her bedroom. She cried and screamed at him to stop, but he was now insane. He tossed Jason aside and went at her again, ripping off all her clothes. Almost naked, embarrassed, and ashamed, my mom crawled to her room and locked the door while Jason found new strength to restrain dad. My father staggered off to the garage for more drink and cigarettes.

I was in shock and knew that this was going to be a long night. I made a plan and announced, "Daniel, Sarah, Kyle, we're going on a field trip. Everything is going to be okay, trust me, and do what I say, please. I'm taking you to Veronica's house tonight. Let's go."

I grabbed their backpacks and loaded their school outfits for the next day. Veronica was a trusted family friend who lived less than a mile away. I called to give her a heads up and she invited us over with open arms. She knew my parents well and knew how sick dad was.

I continued barking orders. "Jason, stay here and make sure that dad doesn't go crazy again. Hopefully, he'll just pass out. I'm counting on you. I'll be back soon. Please protect our mother."

I gathered the kids, and we walked to Veronica's house. I dropped them off and said I would be back soon. I told her what was going on and asked her to watch over the children. She was a good friend to us, and I thank her for that. The walk home in the dark after what had just happened was hard. So many thoughts and questions ran through my mind. *What the heck just happened? What in the hell is happening? Why is dad so crazy? Why did he almost kill mom? Why is he so mean? I want a normal family and childhood. I want a normal father.*

Disbelief, shock, surprise, horror, and sadness all hit me at once. I felt overwhelmed with emotions that I didn't understand and couldn't control. As I turned the corner and headed up our cul-de-sac street, I said aloud, "Why are all the pumpkins my brothers, sister, and I carved all smashed in the cul-de-sac? What's this smashed clay ceramic stuff? Oh my God, these are things my mom made throughout her life. These are things she put her heart, soul, and time into painting." I walked around the street and gathered some of the broken objects. My heart sank. I couldn't breathe. I grew angrier and felt a deep rage. "He did this. What a heartless person. I hate him. I will never forgive him. He will never change."

Lying on the cold rock on the side of Mount Rosalie, I wondered: *Why was I thinking about my family and what I would say to them if I had another chance?* It was obvious I had nothing good to say about my dad, but I did have many questions for him. *Why wasn't my childhood normal? Why wasn't he a loving father? Why was I never good enough? Why did he never accept me? Why was he always drunk? Why was he so violent? Why did he have five kids if all we did was make him miserable?*

My father was never my role model. He acted disengaged at home, and I despised him throughout my childhood. He never spent quality father-daughter time with me. He worked hard to put food on our table, but his drunkenness, screaming, fighting, and violence trumped that. I never heard the words "I love you," and never got a hug. I never did anything good enough for him.

Living outside of normal society, he was unable to say anything nice to anyone except his workmates and drinking buddies. When I was young, I tried to win his approval. I wanted him to be proud of me. That's all I really wanted. As I grew up, his comments to me only became more negative. I resented him, and then finally hated him. I tried to win my father's acceptance and approval. It took me years to realize that I'll never have the father I wanted.

At some point, we stop investing energy in a toxic relationship. People deserve to be treated well, especially by those who are supposed to love them. We need to avoid those who hurt us. Life is too short to grieve for something we will never have. I wanted my father's approval. I wanted his love. I wanted to love him. But all he does is hurt me, and I made the choice to save myself. I realized that I can't change him, so it's better that we part ways. I wish it was different, but the past cannot be changed. My father can no longer hurt me if I no longer let him.

Shaking from the cold and my nightmare of memories, I refocused on my current situation. Closing my eyes and remembering the past wasn't going to get me off the mountain. As I shivered in the icy wind, I knew why that memory had come back to me. I could still remember that incident like it happened yesterday.

I moved my hands back to the slab and tried to adjust my position. Ouch! The painkiller from Prakash hadn't worked. I rolled my head to the other side and sagged deeper into the mountain.

# Chapter 5 – "High" School

Before I attended high school, my life headed in a downward direction. In middle school, I made bad choices, hanging out with the wrong crowd. I felt that all of my safe places were tainted, especially my home. I figured that if my parents exhibited ridiculous behavior, I would too. I was sick of being the parent to them, my brothers and sister and trying to solve all the family's issues. I was giving my strength and energy away, and getting nothing in return.

Despite my efforts, I was treated like crap. I constantly took care of my brothers and sister. Why did my parents make us go to church, and then do the things the priest said not to do? If I only knew what the word hypocrite meant back then. I lived with parents who were hypocrites. Their mantra was, "Do what I say, not what I do."

At some point, my energy shifted and Alyson, the rebel, was born. If my parents didn't care about me, then I was finished with them. I was done trying to fix their marriage and our family problems. I was active in sports, but things changed tremendously. At track practice, other rebels and I would run a different route, sneak away, and smoke cigarettes.

Toward the end of middle school, I began drinking and smoking marijuana. The group I ran with was busy stealing cigarettes, make-up, jewelry, and other stuff. It wasn't because we needed these things and couldn't afford them. It was the high of getting away with stolen goods.

Stealing became an addiction until I got caught. That dreadful phone call to my parents was the last thing I wanted. Their anger doubled and I was grounded. But I didn't let that hold me back. My new rush was sneaking out after they went to bed, or bringing friends to my downstairs room where we drank and smoked. Occasionally, we were too loud and woke my father. I know now that my drinking and smoking were unacceptable things to do. I hated that my parents did it to extremes, and then yell and ground me for rebelling.

After I was caught stealing, I didn't take anything for a while, but the bug came back a few months later. The group I hung with went from stealing cigarettes and makeup to bigger items. We went to malls and hit jewelry stores. Jewelry was easy to steal, so we did that on weekends until I was caught again. This time, however, it wasn't just a call to my parents, but a court date, fine, and community service. I was grounded for six months. *Hell no,* I thought. *I'm not going to sit home for the next six months.*

I rebelled against my parents, and I realized that mountain climbing was another type of rebellion. I was rebelling against my bad friends and the peer pressures that bogged me down for so long. I rebelled against other people's expectations. I chose rebellion for my own enrichment and self-discovery. With this choice, however, there was risk, and my new reality was being confined to this painful position, unable to extricate myself. This time, it might be a death sentence. I was still bleeding internally, and felt my body's remaining warmth disappearing into the wind.

## Downward Bound

I had two groups of friends in high school. The good group were my sports teammates. Laura was in my good group. My bad group were the popular party kids. I didn't know where I belonged. I enjoyed my bad group because it took my mind off my demeaning home life. My bad friends smoked cigarettes, drank booze, and experimented with drugs. My good friends played sports, went to the mall, and watched movies. It was interesting to watch the parents of each group. I associated my good friends with supportive, caring, loving parents, and my bad friends had problems at home like mine.

During my freshman year, I played volleyball, soccer, and made the junior varsity and varsity teams. Whenever anyone got hurt on a varsity team, I filled in, and people learned about me. For the first three years in high school, I was popular enough to be nominated for homecoming queen. It made me feel special that people liked me. It also made me wonder why my father didn't like me.

What people didn't know was that I often met friends in the morning to smoke pot before school, left school at lunch to smoke more pot, and ditched classes to smoke cigarettes and drink. Sometimes I was high or drunk during volleyball and soccer practices. I was definitely downward bound.

As my behavior drifted from bad to worse, a few of the girls knew what was going on, but never said anything to the coaches. They knew my father, felt sorry and sympathetic for me, and helped me hide. Life got worse, and I was spiraling out of control. I became addicted to alcohol, cigarettes, and marijuana, and started learning about other drugs. I was intoxicated with my bad group of friends and got to a point where I couldn't say no to peer pressure. I wanted a way out of my life. I wanted to be accepted by my bad group of friends and was willing to do anything to make that happen.

## Homecoming

The first year I was nominated for homecoming, I was with my older bad friends. Nevertheless, I felt beautiful, and rubbed my arms and felt chills run up and down my body. The queen nominees gathered in a single file line and were about to walk onto the homecoming dance floor in front of everyone. Hundreds of my peers had gathered, along with teachers and coaches.

The door opened, and we walked out. The lights, music, and people were overwhelming. I felt out of control walking into that room. We reached the stage and everyone stared at us, the nominated royalty. We were moments away from seeing who the king and queen were for each class. As I looked out, I saw my volleyball coach, the principal, my math teacher, my parents, classmates, and teammates. Did anyone other than my bad friends know what I was on? Did they know how messed up I was? Why were my parents here?

A few hours before the dance, I had dropped a couple ecstasy pills, smoked pot, and drank too much booze. I was so messed up that I thought I would be arrested, kicked out of school, or taken to the hospital to have my stomach pumped. When people said hi, I muttered hi back, but kept conversations to a minimum.

As I stood on stage in front of everyone, my heart raced until I felt it would jump out of my chest. As music filled the room, the lights made me dizzy, and I wondered if I could remain standing. My classmates had voted; now the MC would announce the winners. He started with the freshman class and worked his way through the grades. When they announced the freshman king and queen, I held my breath. When I wasn't picked, I swayed with relief, since I didn't have to dance in front of everyone.

I spent the next hour at a photo session with the royalty. My volleyball coach found me, and I could barely look him in the eye. I tried to act normal, but wondered if everyone knew. After another hour of royal nonsense, I found my bad friends and we bolted. It was time to party. I couldn't believe I had escaped the dance. I couldn't believe the person I had become. I couldn't say no to my bad friends. I was addicted to drugs, alcohol, and smoking. I was headed downward bound with little hope of getting out.

## Seth

Near the end of my freshman year, I met a handsome boy named Seth. He was a serious rebel, which made him more attractive. Seth and his friends did different drugs, and he sold drugs. One day in English class, Seth had a bottle of liquid acid. Acid alters your mental capacity or worse, and can put you in the hospital or kill you. I naively took a hit of acid on my tongue during class. Taking acid in class? That was the direction I was headed, and things only got worse. "How could I say no to my boyfriend?" My self-confidence and self-esteem dwindle away as I sit in back of the class tripping acid and feel like my brain is leaking out of my ear. I don't think this is normal…

Seth and my bad friends were older than me, and these people accelerated my descent. I easily gave into peer pressure. I got into trouble with the police a few times during high school and often found myself at Saturday cop classes, detention, community service, and paying fines. Eventually, my volleyball coach was so concerned that he started sending me to a school counselor.


## Desi

I played on a softball team called the Sluggers in middle school. One of my teammates was Desi. We went to different schools, but maintained a friendship into high school.

When I was sixteen, a new restaurant opened near my house. I worked there as a hostess, along with my old friend Desi. We started our restaurant journey together, working hard and making money. Soon, after-work parties formed, and we both got fake IDs through a restaurant friend. Clearly, going out with the older crowd after work was the thing to do. Every night we wondered, "Who's having a house party?" or "What bar is everyone going to?"

Occasionally, our general manager closed the restaurant, inviting four or five of us to stay after hours and we would get crazy. He opened the bar and made drinks. We blasted music, sang, and danced. A few times we passed out on the booth seats and the cleaning crew woke us up the next morning.

Desi and I became waitresses when we turned eighteen, and the parties became more serious. Desi dated the general manager and I dated the kitchen manager. Another girl named Stephanie introduced us to cocaine. We learned that many restaurant people used cocaine and, worse, the general manager dealt it.

Cocaine was bad news for me. We had all-night cocaine sessions with friends. Part of my brain disbelieved that I was snorting stuff through my nose. We went into the bathroom during our work shifts to snort lines of coke. I was seriously addicted to drugs and had no will power to say no. I felt like I was in a living nightmare.

I worked at the restaurant for six years, and sank deeper each year. The restaurant crowd became my family and the restaurant was my home away from home. Booze, drugs, and partying numbed my emotions and feelings. I learned how to take drugs, but never learned how to deal with emotions and feelings. I continued my downward trajectory. My desire to play sports dwindled, since sports cut into time I could spend with friends doing drugs and getting into trouble.

## Lies

With my double life, I pretended to be two different people depending on whom I was around. I lied constantly to get out of trouble, get what I wanted, and to spare other people's feelings. Like stealing, I lied to see what I could get away with. I learned lying from my father, a master of the art of twisting reality. He lives in a world of his own beliefs, whether they are real or not. I learned how to lie from him, so eventually lying became natural and easy.

I could tell a lie and believe it with such conviction that I would sometimes think the lie was true. Without knowing it, I was tangled in a web of self-deception.

Hours had passed, and I was still lying on the cold snowy slab. Reality slapped me back to the increasing possibility that I could die here. No lie could save me from blood loss and hypothermia. Most of the loss was internal, and there wasn't much I could do about that. Hypothermia is insidious, and continued to creep into me. A ground rescue might not reach me before death, but that was out of my control. I couldn't lie about my injuries, the storm, or the fact that it was now night. The temperature continued to drop, and rescue was still hours away. Normally, we talk about feeling this or that, but my reality was that I felt my broken body less and less. I now moved just to see if my pain was still there.

I strongly felt God's presence on the mountain. I felt my friend Chris beside me. The signal from beyond was clear. If I survive this, I have to change and be a new person. I told myself that I could make a difference in people's lives. Not too long ago, I had been on a 50-mile run with my Chris and told him my dream of writing a book and becoming a motivational speaker or something in the field of inspiring and motivating others. He inspired me. He encouraged me and told me that I could do it and gave me the confidence in myself to believe that I really could.

I begged the snowy sky for forgiveness. I wanted the forgiveness of others for the bad things I had done many years ago, and for all of my anger, resentment, and hate. I wanted to start by learning how to forgive myself. *I have to make it because I have a purpose in my life that has not yet been fulfilled.* I prayed.

*God, give me strength to endure what's ahead. Give me a chance to help others by telling my story.* That would make my suffering worthwhile. Can we ever be truly happy if we have never been sad? I have been truly sad, and my sadness belongs to the past. I want it behind me. I want to be happy and take my place in this world. I have learned so much on the side of this mountain. *I am cold, so scared, and so alone. Help me.*

# Chapter 6 – Jail

"Prakash, I don't think I can handle the pain if they move me without morphine. I've been here for hours, frozen and bleeding. The thought of being moved makes me cringe. Sometimes, I want to die before they get here so I don't have to endure the pain."

For my entire life I had always found a way to not feel pain. It usually consisted of drugs or alcohol. Now, I was facing the most severe, intense form of pain a person could imagine, and I had to do it without drugs. I didn't know if I could do it. I didn't know how to do it.

"Alyson, these guys are a super professional outfit. I'm sure they'll come prepared. If not morphine, I'm sure they'll bring something else that's good. Let's not think about that and try to live in the moment."

"What if they try to move me and I can't endure the pain? What if the pain kills me?"

"Alyson, pain won't kill you, but staying here will. Have you ever heard the saying, 'God will never give you more than you can handle'?"

"No, I haven't heard that saying. I sure hope it's true though. I'm getting really cold and can't feel my feet."

Prakash re-fluffed the down jacket around my feet and moved snow off me. Even though the snow was insulating, it would eventually melt from my body heat, soak my clothes, and accelerate my demise. I told Prakash that there was a waterproof pant shell in my pack. He pulled it out and spread it across my legs to keep them dry.

We continued talking about other warm places, including Australia, Tahiti, Mexico, and the Samoan Islands. Prakash taught me an energizing breathing technique that helped. I sang songs to pass the time and Prakash provided a howling accompaniment.

The snow became heavier, and Prakash reminded me to breathe deep and relax. I would take four deep breaths but then start panting. I continued to lose blood internally and was slowly bleeding to death. I closed my eyes and traveled back to my past life, but Prakash wouldn't let me doze for long to make sure I was alive and breathing. He kept moving to stay warm, and then vanished for long periods of time to look for the rescue team. My positive attitude was fading. I closed my eyes and went back to my inner thoughts.

I opened my eyes. My head was pounding and I was shivering. I looked up at the concrete ceiling. I turned my head and looked around the room. I had no idea where I was. It was a small room with no windows. I asked, "How did I get here?" I looked down and saw Desi lying on concrete, stretched out on a blanket. "Desi, what's going on? Where are we?"

"It's about time you woke up. You've been passed out cold for a day."

"What happened?"

"Well, Alyson. We're in jail. We got arrested Friday morning, and the judge will not be back until Monday morning. We have to stay here all weekend."

"Why am I in my bathing suit in jail?"

It was a spring break trip to Lake Havasu during our junior year in high school. I was with Desi, Bridget, and Bonnie. We had fake IDs and had lied to our parents about where we were going. Our first year at Lake Havasu was so much fun that we had to come back. The road trip began with a blizzard in Denver, but we would not let anything stop us. We drove from Denver to Lake Havasu City and got to our hotel late Thursday night. We checked into the room, and started drinking. It was already two in the morning, but the halls, bars, and streets were packed with people.

Already tipsy, we started meeting people and had a blast. At five o'clock in the morning, Bridget and Bonnie called it a night and went back to the hotel, but Desi and I were just getting started. Well, at least I was, and Desi wouldn't leave me alone because she knew I could get into trouble. Who needed sleep when there was drinking to do? A group of guys with a boat invited us to go cliff diving when the sun came up. Boating, cliff diving, and drinking sounded great. We grabbed swim gear, more beer, and headed to the dock with the guys. I was so intoxicated that I could barely walk, and my muddled speech made little sense. Somehow, I got into my bathing suit.

We hopped onto the boat, but before we launched, there was a commotion on the beach, and a few guys started to fight. Three police officers arrived and broke it up. The cops asked for IDs, but before I could hand them my fake ID, Desi grabbed it from my hand and hid it. Even without an ID, I was busted. It was obvious that I was underage and drunk. I had to take a Breathalyzer test, and after I blew, the policemen could not believe that I was still standing. Desi also had to blow, and she was over the legal limit too. They apologized to Desi but said that due to my condition and the fact that she was underage and over the limit, they were taking us to jail.

"You're in your bathing suit because that's what you got arrested in. It's Saturday night, and we were arrested yesterday morning. You passed out once we got here and have been out cold since."

We sat in the concrete jail cell all weekend, waiting to see the judge. It was awful. The half white, half wheat bologna sandwiches served to us were disgusting.

We saw the judge on Monday morning. We each had one phone call and needed $1,000 for bail. There was no way I was going to call my parents. I had lied about where I was going, so to call from jail would be the end of me. Desi called her mom and she bailed us out of jail. An underage drinking ticket, bail, and probation rocketed this trip down the drain.

"How did I get here?" For a moment, I didn't know if I was in jail or on the mountain. I realized that the memory of waking up in my bathing suit on a hard board in jail was similar to my current plight. Ten years later, I asked the same question again, and answered it.

It was February, I was in a blizzard, and immobile with broken bones. Unlike jail, I could die here. There would be no bologna sandwich. Worse, there was no judge to let me go with just a ticket and bail money. No amount of money could beam me away from the slab. I was cold, stuck, and hopeless.

"Prakash, do you think you could snap my broken bone back into place and take me down the mountain?"

Prakash answered, "I don't want to try that when we're suspecting a pelvic and maybe even spinal fracture. We should wait this out, Alyson. The rescuers will be here."

"What if we call SAR and someone can guide you through the process over the phone?"

To satisfy my pleas, Prakash called SAR again, and the official reply was, "Oh no, please don't, the rescuers should be there soon."

# Chapter 7 – End Of The Road

Why was I in so many bad relationships? Not just relationships with guys, but any relationship. It wasn't until I started running and mountain climbing that I began developing meaningful and deep friendships. These were the relationships I had always wanted. The bad friend relationships were almost the end of me. They felt impossible to break free from because I had so little self-confidence.

Why do some teenage girls hate their mothers? When I was young, I loved my mom. I felt sad about everything she went through with my father. When I was a teenager and in my early twenties, I began to hate her. She always told me what to do and never let me be myself. In my teenage years, I didn't feel sorry for her, and grew angry because she never divorced my father and made us go through so much pain. I was angry because she let my father treat her badly and she never stood up for herself. I felt like screaming at her, "Mom. Part of getting stepped on is lying down. Get divorced. Do us all a favor, mom." I became estranged from my parents, and had to learn from their bad examples. I learned that when you don't take a stand for what's right, nobody else will do it for you. When children are involved, they are the ones who suffer.

## Graduation

I played soccer and volleyball in my senior year. I had played both sports for over five years, but by my senior year the thought of another season made me sick. I was good at both sports, and felt that if I had invested more energy, I could have received college scholarships and continued to play. But it wasn't worth it to me anymore. I was speeding down a bad road. I still wanted to do something with my life, but my addictions wanted more party time.

Neither of my parents went to college. They didn't push me to go, and they would certainly not pay for it. So, the thought of going to school when nobody cared—and having to pay for it myself—wasn't appealing.

After high school graduation, the thought of having more time with my restaurant and school friends sounded a lot easier than going to college. With dwindling school spirit, I finished my senior season playing soccer and volleyball. The season ended in December, and I had the spring to do whatever I wanted. I had only one close friend who went to college after graduation. Otherwise, nobody I knew did. My father always told me that he started his company and made money without a college degree. For him, college was a waste of money and time.

Don't your parents know best, and don't they want the best for their children? Maybe, but in my case, going to college would make my father angrier than he already was. I was ready to push his beliefs aside, but I knew that, aside from having to pay for it, I needed a burning desire to make it through college. That spring, I waited for a desire to go to college, but it never came. My desire for drinking, drugs, and partying grew stronger.

I had no set idea about what I wanted to do after high school. My main motivation was to get a job that made decent money so I could get out of my parent's house and into my own place. It was time to separate from my parents. My waitress job at the restaurant didn't pay well, but I could squeak by. However, I knew that I couldn't be a waitress forever, and would soon have to make decisions about what I wanted to do with my life.

On the morning of my high school graduation, my little brother Daniel and I drank a 1.75-liter bottle of Southern Comfort. We thought we should start drinking early so we could have fun on this special day. It's my high school graduation; shouldn't I be celebrating? I associated celebrating with drugs and alcohol. It was what I had seen growing up so why wouldn't I continue with what I was accustom to others in my life doing when they were celebrating something? The "Comfort" was in before ten-thirty a.m., and then it was time to meet friends before my graduation. I had a celebratory session with good weed before the ceremony. After the booze and weed, I was in bad shape, but I thought, "What are they going to do to me now? Kick me out of school? Good luck, because I'm done."

We made it to the ceremony completely wasted. It was a hot May afternoon and the bleachers were full of parents, friends, and family eager to see their (presumably sober) sons and daughters graduate. My parents and family were there too. I sat with my classmates, wore the cap and gown, and waited for my name to be called. The principal worked through the alphabet and soon reached the Ks. My glorious moment arrived, but when the principal called my name, I wasn't sure if I could stand up, much less walk onto the stage. Breathing deeply, I switched into athlete mode and grabbed my diploma. I shook hands with the principal and teachers, then exhaled my last high school breath. I officially made it through high school.

Now it was time for graduation parties. After the ceremony, I headed back to my parent's house where they threw a graduation party for me. Friends and family came, and it was a good time. I sneaked drinks while mingling with the guests. By mid-afternoon, I was a soggy mess. My parents knew that I was drinking, but they were well on their way to their own demise.

After the sports season ended in December, I drank more than ever and gained weight throughout the spring. I was also smoking too much pot, and smoked a pack of cigarettes a day. Both of my parents also smoked a pack a day, so I had always been around it. Monkey see, monkey do. By spring, I had gained 65 pounds and weighed close to 210 pounds. My normal weight throughout high school had been from 145 to 150 pounds. I was fat but, with my ability to twist the truth, I didn't admit to myself that I was fat. I was messed up on a variety of fronts, and I didn't know who I was anymore. I didn't look in the mirror and see Alyson. Little Alyson hadn't just grown up, she was gone. I was in a stranger's body doing alien things that had nothing to do with the "authentic" Alyson.

My mom said something to me at my graduation party that I would never forget. Her blunt words that night are still with me, and these words turned me in a good direction. At the time, I hated her for saying it. I thought she was being mean and hurtful, and I couldn't believe she would say such awful things to her daughter.

My mom looked me in the eye, and said, "Alyson, you've really let yourself go. Your face looks like a swarm of bees have stung you and you're more than 50 pounds overweight. What has happened to you? You're a complete mess, you're a drunk, and you're fat."

Overwhelmed by disbelief, I started swearing at her and calling her names. Who was she to tell me I'm a drunk? Where does she think I learned this behavior? I left the house with my friends and went to other parties. I didn't talk to my mom for quite a while after graduation night. Her words were true, but they hurt me deeply. It's also true that my parents never had any idea how to talk to us effectively. How could they when their communication to one another consisted of yelling and screaming? They usually blurted the blunt truth to each other with screams. There was no reason to lighten the words even if they may hurt someone. Nevertheless, the words my mom said to me that night planted a seed in my head that something was wrong. Something was wrong with me. What was I doing? Where was I headed? How do I get out of this mess?

Without opening my eyes, I knew that these questions were with me on the mountain. *What was I doing? Where was I headed? How did I get here?* Most important, *How do I get out of this mess?* My current circumstances were completely different from anything I had experienced before, but I still asked the same questions. I could not blame my parents for the slab or storm, but it was time for answers. The easy chopper ride had failed, and I now knew that the answers before me all involved my strength, power, passion, and will to live. I cannot die. I must not die. I will not die.

"Just hang on. Breathe. Hang on. Breathe. Alyson, Alyson, Alyson. Just hang on!"

## Real Estate

During my senior year, I dated a guy named David whose mom was the senior broker at a real estate firm. David sold real estate too, and that gave me the idea that, maybe after high school, I could work in real estate. I was tall, outgoing, good looking, and energetic. The real estate industry sounded perfect.

I decided to attend real estate school and get a real estate license. People in the field made good money, and I thought, "Why can't I do that instead of waiting tables?" Real Estate College was a six-month class to prepare me for the real estate exam that I had to pass to get my license. I saved money waiting tables and paid for the school. During class, I met new people, and it felt like this was a good avenue for me. The final exam was two separate tests that cost $100 apiece. I had to pass both tests to get a license, but I could take either test as many times as I wanted. However, every time I repeated a test, I had to pay another $100. It took me six tries to pass both tests. I wouldn't give up. I never quit anything, even bad things. It's in my personality to finish things and then celebrate, so I had a cooler full of beer in the car to commemorate my passage. I launched my new career by blasting myself completely out of control.

I continued to wait tables after I signed on with a real estate firm. I tried hard to get things going in the real estate field, but it was difficult to be an 18-year-old girl with no experience. I had trouble getting people to trust me with hundreds of thousands of dollars. I tried to be an independent broker for a year, but didn't get anywhere. My drinking and drug use still spiraled. By age 20, I hit 220 pounds and thought, "Why would anyone want to buy or sell their house through a fat drunk?"

Trust me!

I moved from place to place to escape my parents, both of whom I now hated. Look what they had done to me. Look at my childhood. How could anybody go through that kind of childhood and turn out normal, successful, or anything other than a complete mess? I liked to blame people for my misfortunes, and never wanted to take responsibility for my actions or choices. This is a behavior I learned from my father. He always blamed others for why he had to drink, why he broke something, why he punched a hole in the wall, why he treated us the way he did. There was always a reason and someone to blame other than himself. Was I destined to be like him?

Desi and I got an apartment together for a year. I had multiple fake IDs, hung out with the older crowd, and partied like I had been doing for the last four years. I was now 20 years old. Sports had been my saving grace, but they were now gone. I had no way to numb my emotions except with booze and drugs. My downward bound was now in free fall, and I had no rope.

## Over the Cliff

It was another evening after working in the restaurant, followed by bars and house parties. By this point, I was a chronic alcoholic. I've never been able to have one or two drinks. My personality is all or nothing. I do things in excess. That's how I've always been, and drinking, drugs, and cigarettes were not good things to be addicted to.

I don't remember that night well. I woke up in my parent's front yard with my mom shaking me and crying, "Alyson, Alyson! What are you doing? Are you okay? Wake up."

It was five a.m. on a weekday, and my mom was headed to work. She found me outside lying in the grass surrounded by my own vomit and a few other nasty things. I had a black eye and bruises all over my body. My car was at a crazy angle in the middle of the cul-de-sac. I had blacked out behind the wheel, and had somehow crawled to my parent's front yard. The story was that I had taken a bad fall at a house party the night before, and that's where I got the black eye and bruises. Yeah, right. My mom wasn't ashamed of me, she was afraid for my life. I couldn't keep living like this.

Party Girl

## Too Many Parties

I stumbled inside and passed out on the downstairs couch. I woke up later with another pounding hangover. I made it to the bathroom, looked in the mirror, and could not believe what I saw. "I'm done. I can't keep doing this." Two years ago, my mom told me that I was fat. I was now 20 pounds heavier. I didn't need my mom telling me I would end up killing myself or someone else if I kept falling.

There is always a ground somewhere to stop you, and I felt mine rushing up to meet me. I needed an intervention. I needed to make life-changing actions because no one else was going to do it for me. Stripped raw, I knew I was better than this. I knew in my heart what I could do, and I knew what God wanted from me. God knew I was special and going to do big things with my life.

# Echo Lake

I didn't have to work, so I took off toward the mountains. I wasn't sure where I was going or what I was doing. I just drove. After a couple of hours, I was in the Front Range and saw a sign for Echo Lake. I took the turn, and arrived at a place I had never been before. It was beautiful.

I parked my car close to the lake and inhaled the clean air. No smoke in sight. I saw the reflection of high mountains shimmering on the lake. My mind was alive. Who needs drugs? Tall pine trees surrounded the lake and I found their smell intoxicating. Who needs booze? I started walking on a trail that looked like it would circle the lake. I felt at peace. Who needs to party? I felt like I was in a new home.

I never went to the mountains with my family, so this was a new experience. I felt a change happening to me. I walked for hours, found other trails and walked them. I disappeared into thoughts about my life and how I was going to change for the better.

I thought, "I know my childhood was lousy. I know that two alcoholics raised me. I know I was mentally and emotionally abused for most of my life. I know that I can feel sorry for myself and keep heading down this road, or I can change and take a stand for myself."

I knew the time had come to make positive, life-altering changes. My pity party was taking me down, but my past didn't define who I was. I defined who I was. At any moment, I could change my road and be who I wanted to be. I was ready for Alyson to change her life. I wanted the authentic Alyson back, I wanted to meet authentic Alyson.

I lay on my slab listening to the wind howling through the storm like a pack of wolves. I thought, *"The ugly years of my life sent me to where I am now. I'm on a mountain with something broken in my body, not knowing if I'm going to live or die, internally bleeding to death, and becoming hypothermic. It's crazy to think that ten years ago I almost killed myself with drinking and drugs. Now look where I am and how I might die. Unbelievable."* I was trying to change things and be a better person, and then this. Life can't end here.

I never knew how strong I was until being strong was the only option I had to save my life. I shuddered to think about those ugly years, and pushed them from my mind. I was no longer that person. I had learned much in my short life, and it could not have been in vain. There had to be a purpose for going through it all. The ugliness of the past had made me a better person. I was still fighting it, and fighting for my life again, but this time, all I could do was wait. This time, I desperately needed help.

# Chapter 8 – Evolution

## Floating, floating, floating

*If I shut my eyes and go to sleep maybe God will take me while I'm sleeping. That won't be as painful as enduring what lies ahead with a rescue, and then I can be out of this mess.* Wait. A second inner voice spoke. *Alyson, this kind of thinking is going to kill you. Be positive and stay positive. If you live, what will you do differently with your life? What would you do with a second chance?*

I still lay in the snowy cold and still had hours to reflect on my life. What would you do differently if you had a second chance at life? Have you ever asked yourself that? Of course, we ask ourselves these questions often enough wondering what we might do differently "if," but this wasn't just a hypothetical question. It was a real question and now it was up to me to have real answers. I started to form a vow to myself.

*If I live through this, I vow to live authentically even if that means not doing what people want me to do, or what society influences me to do. I need to embrace what sparks my soul. I need to cherish my passions, especially those that give meaning to my existence. If I live, I vow to live my life as it should be lived. I vow to trust myself and my instincts. I vow to cherish each moment I am given. I vow to do what I can to make this a better place and to help others on this journey.*

With these assertions, I thought back to my old life and all that had led me to this moment.

## Following My Feet

After my spiritual awakening at Echo Lake, I knew I was ready to evolve. Where could I begin? Change is never easy. It's what many of us fight on a daily basis. I knew that fear of change can be paralyzing, and I couldn't let that happen. I had to relax and try.

This change was intense. I had been addicted to drugs, alcohol, smoking, and partying for many years of my life. It's what I knew how to do best. It's how I coped with life's ups and downs, how I had fun, how I got in trouble; it defined me. I wasn't sure how to break free from these addictions. I knew it would be incredibly hard and I would have to summon inner strength if I were to really achieve becoming a new person; a healthier person.

I followed my feet to the gym. It was my first time at the gym in a couple of years. I used to run regularly during soccer and volleyball, but now I was in sad shape. I stepped onto a treadmill and set it to 6, which equated to a 10-minute-per-mile pace. I thought, "I will do one mile at a 10-minute pace and see how that goes."

It seemed okay at first, but I was soon out of breath. There was no way I could hold that pace for a mile. I couldn't even do it for 30 seconds. I immediately decreased the speed, started walking, and began coughing uncontrollably. Not coughing because I was sick, but coughing because of how much I had smoked. How could I consider running when I couldn't even breathe for one minute at a measly 10 minute per mile pace? I was so embarrassed that I looked around the gym to make sure there was no one there I knew. What had happened to me in the past few years? I used to be one of the good athletes in my high school. Now, I'm a fat smoker who can't run.

I finished my mile walking slowly, and decided to call it good for the day. Trying to not get too discouraged, I turned the treadmill off, stood there for a few moments, and then turned to step off the back. What I saw surprised me. Alicia, one of my old friends from high school, was on the elliptical machine behind me. I had a falling out with Alicia toward the end of high school, and our friendship foundered on bad terms. I stared at her, and she looked amazing. She was skinny, in shape, happy, and healthy. She stared at me, and I think she was in disbelief.

Alicia and I were both nominated for homecoming queen three years in a row. She beat me two of the years, so I had always felt a little competitive and wanted to beat her. Now, seeing Alicia and how good she looked made me feel even worse about myself. I couldn't imagine what she was thinking about me. She was probably wondering how I had become so fat. Maybe I was so fat and different that she didn't even know who I was. That was not likely. I knew she remembered me. Without a word, I grabbed my stuff and left as fast as I could.

After that day at the gym, I wanted revenge. Not revenge on Alicia, revenge on the person I had become. I was going to get my revenge on the fat Alyson and show Alicia what the real Alyson was really capable of. Never again did I want to experience that feeling of total failure.

## My Epiphany

I knew that real change only occurs when the person is ready and willing, and has defined their change. When someone else demands a change, it never seems to work. My father repeatedly told my mom that she was the alcoholic and the root cause to all the problems in their marriage. If she would quit drinking, their life would be a hundred times better. My father always seemed to feel that other people were responsible for all his problems and that if they changed their problematic behaviors, his life would be problem free. I knew that I couldn't let this crazy lifestyle define who I was going to be. I was better than that. Just because both of my parents were alcoholics and most of my friends were worse than that didn't mean that's what I had to do or who I had to be.

When I was finally able to take my own reins and have the courage to say that I have a choice, I knew I could do anything and be anyone I wanted to be. At first, it was hard to make changes. I knew I had to get out of the restaurant industry because nothing good would come out of it, especially at my current restaurant. I started by fixing my resume and looking at jobs in real estate. I applied to many different places and eventually landed a job at Richmond Homes. I was excited. This would be a big step in my new direction.

Once I had secured the job, I quit the restaurant. It wasn't easy, but I accepted that if I wanted to change my life, I had to stop associating with bad friends. I took a mental inventory of my real friends. I had a list of about 25 from high school and the restaurant. Then, I wondered, if I stopped drinking, smoking, and partying, would I have any friends left? When I subtracted my alcoholic and drug-addicted friends, the list dropped to three. Yikes. I had three people in my life that I could consider real friends since they didn't have to drink, smoke, or party.

I needed to increase the number of real friends and the best way to do that was to have other hobbies. I was always athletic and into sports, and I missed the competitiveness. I didn't want to play soccer or volleyball on recreational teams, so I wasn't sure what to do. I realized that I wouldn't be part of anything until I lost weight and got back into shape.

My new moves were hard, but I worked at them slowly. Leaving the restaurant was a great step. My real estate job was in a new home community, and there were four of us who worked there. This job focused my time and thoughts in a better direction. There were no more weekend parties because I worked weekends when real estate sales are the busiest. I wanted a serious career, and working hard pulled me away from my earlier addictions. I also wanted to focus on losing weight and getting into other activities. I was now 21 years old, and I threw away all my old fake IDs. I didn't want to give up drinking completely, but I did want to drink in moderation. How many alcoholics have said that, and then failed? I knew this would be extremely difficult for me, but I would try. Cold turkey, I quit smoking cigarettes, and this was the best single thing I did for my health. I knew that I had to quit smoking if I wanted to get back into shape. After seeing Alicia at the gym, I was motivated. No more coughing. Well, at least not as much.

## Treadmill Time

I was never into running on a treadmill at the gym. We always did our running outside for soccer and around the gym for volleyball. In comparison, a treadmill is boring. However, I needed some numbers to keep track of my progress, and a treadmill with a computer was good for that. Since my treadmill was indoors, I could never make excuses for not working out because of the weather. Also, my treadmill's controlled environment reduced my chances of injury which was a serious concern since I was so heavy and putting so much extra stress on my joints.

This was hard. The first thing I learned was that I was in worse shape than I thought. I was an odious 70 pounds overweight and it hurt to run. My muscles immediately became sore, and I couldn't afford a massage therapist. My progress on the treadmill crept like a worm trying to dig a 20-mile tunnel. However, I had quit smoking, and I started to feel small positive results. I was sick of coughing and vowed that, even if it took a year, there would be no more coughing.

I forged a plan to run on my treadmill at least five days a week. Then, strangely, my addictive personality seized this new direction, and I was hell bent to do it. After two months on my treadmill, I was able to jog two miles at an 11 minute per mile pace. This was only a little more than a fast walk, but I was getting both feet into the air at the same time. I knew this speed wouldn't even qualify me for a middle school track team, but I also knew that this was faster and farther than I had been able to do two months earlier.

It was easy to look back at all the mistakes I had made and feel deep regret about my bad choices. I had to focus on moving forward and staying positive. What was regretting my mistakes going to do for me? Absolutely nothing. I tried to stay positive and told myself that maybe the mistakes I regretted were building blocks to help me become the woman I knew I could be. I had to stay focused on improving, not regretting.

After four months, I was able to jog four miles at a nine minute per mile pace. I had sped up and doubled my distance. Patience was winning. I was still far from the track team, but they were not here in the gym to judge my progress. The great day came when I went outside and discovered I could shuffle past the casual walkers on the bike path.

I had been successful in cutting my drinking way down and had also improved my diet. After six months of steady gym visits, I looked and felt better. Nothing spurs progress better than progress. I never shied away from the scale. I had lost 30 pounds in six months. On my do-it-myself program, I was happy and proud. I started turning sideways to look in the mirror. I knew much work remained, but I was headed in the right direction.

Even though my treadmill was getting old, I stayed on it. I was obsessed. After a full year, I could run six miles at an 8:30 per mile pace. I could now say that I was running and not just jogging. Better, I was down 55 pounds, almost back to my old high school weight. I felt great, and I started doing small skips for joy. Now, when I saw people fatter than me, I felt like a heroic stud.

My real estate job was going well. I was learning all the ins and outs of the industry and, for the first time, I felt somewhat passionate about a job and, possibly, a career. Could it be that I was growing up?

More important, I was selective about the people I hung around with. In the beginning, avoiding my old crowd was one of the toughest things I'd had to do. It started with separating from them. It's easier to do the right thing when you are not with people who drag you down. I had to choose which phone calls and texts to return. Yes, I had to cut people out of my life. For a while, I was lonely and didn't have many friends. This was okay because I knew I was becoming a new woman. I was redesigning myself and starting a new life. I told myself that new friends would eventually come.

## Half Marathon

During my year at the gym, I met many people and made friends with some of them. There was a couple named Mike and Mandy that I regularly saw there. They had been watching my progress and commented on how well they thought I was doing.

One day, after a six-mile run on my treadmill, Mike came up to me, and said, "Hey Alyson, do you want to come run the Old Town Race half marathon with us in Fort Collins?"

Startled, I replied, "Mike, what's a half marathon?"

"It's 13.1 miles of running on an outdoor course. I know you can do it, Aly. I watch you run six miles on this treadmill all the time. Come join us; it will be awesome."

Amazingly, I had never heard of a half marathon. I guess I was too caught up in drinking, drugs, and partying to meet people who would discuss such an event. I pondered Mike's invitation for a few minutes, then thought, *Yes, this was exactly what I needed to try—something new.* I had done sports but never an event like this, and it would surround me with people doing good, healthy things.

I walked over to Mike, and announced, "Mike, I'm totally in. Let's do it. How long do I have before the race?"

"Two months."

I felt my heart take a little jump for joy. "Perfect. How do I sign up?"

I had two months to train and prepare for the whopping distance of 13.1 miles, half of a marathon. It sounded like running around the world. The race was in May, which suddenly seemed like tomorrow. I was a bit nervous, but I felt new juices flowing, and that pushed my training to a higher level. I moved from jogging to running and, when May arrived, I was ready. I had never run a race and was so excited. I had no idea what to expect.

On race day, I drove separately from Mike and Mandy, planning to see them at the starting line. When I arrived, the pre-race atmosphere consumed me. Free shirts, a bag of goodies, and a bus ride to the start. I hopped on the bus and tapped my toes on the floor while it rumbled toward the starting line. I found Mike and Mandy and thanked them for telling me about the race and motivating me to participate in the event. I wished them luck and told them I would see them at the finish line. There were about a hundred other runners there. I was no longer in the gym, and there were no treadmills in sight.

Like me, everyone was excited and focused. We put our hands over our hearts for the pre-race national anthem. Suddenly silent, we got a race countdown. Crack! With the gunshot, we were off.

I was still on my do-it-myself program and only felt competitive with myself. I had one goal in mind, and that was to finish my first half marathon. We started running down Poudre Canyon. The fresh air, the river, the persistent pounding of feet, the sounds of focused breathing, and the rolling views made me feel like I wasn't running. I was part of something larger than myself.

The miles disappeared. In my first race, I discovered the famous runner's high.

Between mile 10 and 11, we entered Fort Collins where I was amazed to see crowds of people lining the course, waving signs and cheering us on. People I didn't know were cheering for me to complete something I had never done before. What a change from my father who always told me that I was doing it wrong. Suddenly, I was doing it right. I sped up. I was already high from running, but another new high washed over me. I dashed across the finish line flush with the high of success. This was a far better high than any I had experienced from booze or drugs. Chest heaving, I now knew that booze and drugs had dulled me. This high elevated me, exalted me.

In the crowd of runners near the finish line, I saw the back of another runner's race bib, and it said, "Full Marathon."

Still a rookie, I asked another runner, "What's a full marathon?"

Smiling, that runner explained that a full marathon was running double our distance or 26.2 miles. My jaw dropped. I could not believe that people could, would, or wanted to do that.

I stammered, "People run 26.2 miles for fun?"

The other runner responded, "Yes, all the time. That's the real goal. This race was for training. You did fine here; you could do it."

I thought I had run around the world, and now I was being encouraged to flap my arms and fly to the moon. Still sweating and puffing, the idea of a full marathon sounded absurd and completely crazy to me.

Still flush with my current success, I replied "I just completed my first half marathon in a little over two hours, 2:02 to be precise. I'll worry about a full marathon later."

By the time my pulse dropped below 100, I was totally hooked. I found Mike and Mandy, and we chatted excitedly about the race and what an enjoyable time we all had. I told them that I wanted to do more, and they told me about several websites that featured running races I might be interested in.

# Authentic Alyson

This was the start of a new Alyson, the authentic Alyson. I knew that I needed new interests to point me in the right direction. Little did I know that my addictive personality would grab running and never let go. I soon checked out running websites, found more half marathons, and entered another one. I was excited to have another race to look forward to. This one was high in the mountains, and I anticipated the fresh air and beauty.

I spent the next year working at real estate, running half marathons, and finding God. In my early twenties, I began building a better life. Bringing athletics back into my life was the missing piece of the puzzle. I was back to my high school weight of 150 pounds, and felt and looked great.

My job finally ended because the community we worked was almost sold out. I found another job in a fancy restaurant and did that job until I found another real estate job. At the restaurant, I became friends with an athletic girl named Sue. We worked out at the same gym, ran, and rode bikes together. It was important to have new friends with healthy interests. Sue taught me that it was possible to go out for dinner, have a drink or two, but not get hammered. However, working back in a restaurant, I became upset that I never went to college to create better career options. I now doubted my father's view that college was a waste of time and money, and knew that I needed to believe in myself.

Not having to live under the same roof as my parents allowed me to find the authentic Alyson. The home abuse of my youth had completely blocked my life force. With my life now in decent shape, I felt a need to mend the relationship with my parents, at least my mom. I wanted to continue moving my life in a richer direction. Part of my feeling was to help my parents by showing them my example of a better healthy life. Part of my need was to dissolve my earlier feelings of hate toward my parents. While I was still learning about life, I knew that hate was a poison. It was my emotion and, as long as I hung onto it, it was hurting me. Also, with eyes now open, I believed that everyone deserved a second chance. A larger question loomed. Could I ever forgive my father? Sadly, my parents continued to fight and when I went back to my parent's house, I was on a slippery slope.

Over time, I developed a better relationship with my mother, but my father was impossible. My father had always been emotionally removed and it appeared that he always would be. With urging from me, and with the children grown, my mother finally had the confidence to divorce my father. When she told me she was going to serve him divorce papers, my old fears roared back. I was sure that this would flip his switch, and that he might kill my mother. Forget forgiveness, did I need to call the cops?

With the reality of divorce papers in his lap, my father finally blinked. He told my mom that he was willing to try to change and that he would get counseling. Also important, he said that he would quit drinking. At this point, I knew more about this than my father, and I didn't believe he could do it. Even if he did quit drinking for a while, he would remain a "dry drunk," still exhibiting destructive, addictive behavior. I now also better understood my father, and realized that his statements about changing were his last-ditch efforts to hang onto his control over my mother. Deep down, he was the same person. With this realization, another old wound began to ache again. My father would never accept or even nod to the authentic Alyson. He would never be proud of me.

A sharp shiver shot through my freezing body. *My father would never be proud of me. Worse, if I survived this ordeal, he would tell me that climbing is stupid, unproductive, and a waste of time. Worse still, he would probably tell me that I should have expected what happened to me.*

Flush with sadness, I tried to sputter that my father, since he had none, knew nothing about passion, but that only brought my pain out from under its hiding place. Ugh. Paralyzed by pain, I knew that negative thoughts about my father were not going to get me through this ordeal. Even positive thoughts about my father would not get me through this ordeal, and he was certainly not going to magically appear in tonight's storm to save me. I could hear him saying that anybody stupid enough to climb a mountain, not to mention in the winter, got what they deserved. I could hear him ask why I could never be normal. What is normal? Isn't it better to be who I am than to pretend to be what I am not? Why can't he see that? Why can't I accept that he will never approve of me or the life I have chosen?

I glanced into the dark, the continuing storm, and saw that JB was curled tightly in his life-saving ball. Prakash scanned the night for any sign of the rescuers. Immobile, my thoughts of the past were still in control.

The looming questions of forgiveness swirled in the wind. In or out of the circle, could I forgive my father? Could he forgive me? Did one depend on the other? Could one exist without the other? Earlier, when I tried to forgive my father, my effort had failed. Now, spinning with pain, sadness, and confusion, I discovered a truth. For me, forgiveness had to be a one-way street. I could forgive my father deep in my soul, but I did not have to force him to accept it. It sparked in my brain that, since he could not accept me, he could not accept my forgiveness. I was outside his circle. I could not lie on my death slab wishing I had worked more on my relationship with my father. I could forgive him and be at peace with it. I had to learn how to let go.

When I tried to roll my head, I couldn't. Was my neck frozen? Broken? No, there had to be a simpler reason. With pain and effort, I pulled my mittened right hand up to investigate. Ice. Much of my face and most of my parka hood was crusted over with ice. It had formed from my warm breath freezing. At least the ice was proof that I was still breathing. Squeezing my nose and pawing with my mitten, I flaked it off, being careful that it didn't fall inside my jacket. When I finally managed to roll my head, I had another surprise.

I was in worse physical shape than I had imagined. Every ounce of my body hurt in ways that I could not believe. I had no idea that a person could be in this much pain and still be alive. Any movement of my legs was absolute agony. My physical reality was dismal, and continuing to worsen. I wondered which I was: the body or the thoughts. Maybe it is a combination. *If one dies, does the other? Can our thoughts live on after our body dies? Good grief. Does it matter anymore?*

# Chapter 9 – Passion

Somehow, seconds had turned into hours. The hours had long since wrapped my brain in fear and now, barely able to roll my neck, I felt that my fear blanket was in control. Logic demanded that I remain strong and positive about survival but, with my swirling fear-infested thoughts, bleeding, and hypothermia, my grip on logic was about gone. I felt like a climber who has lost contact with the mountain. Even a blast of logic did not help.

*Why would random strangers from a search and rescue team risk their lives to save mine? How could they find me in the middle of the night in this whiteout? Even if they did find me, how could they move me down six miles to the trailhead? The nearest trail is a mile and a half below. Large boulders and new snow surround me. I don't know what's broken in my body. All I know is that since Prakash got me settled, I've barely moved an inch. Still, when I move even the slightest, pain bombs my brain. Six miles down the mountain in this storm? That would be impossible.*

Optimism is an emotion and my chances of getting out alive were locked in a downward spiral. Even if they get to me, it seemed hopeless.

Prakash was up and moving again to stay warm, and he kept looking for any sign of the rescue team. Bless him. Grimly, I held my phone. I was not supposed to use it unless it was the search and rescue dispatcher. I could only imagine what was going on in the outside world. By now, my friend Shawn, whom I had called earlier in the day, had probably called my husband, and he would have called my family. *My family. I could die and not say goodbye to them.* My grip on my phone tightened.

Working hard in my brain to stay in touch with reality, I sat there while my phone rang and rang. My little sister Sarah called, my little brother Kyle called, and my mom called. By now they all knew what was going on, but they were probably in disbelief. They were hoping I would pick up the phone and announce that whatever Josh told them was a mistake. Each time the phone rang, my heart sank deeper like a rock into a bottomless mineshaft. The phone became another torment. I could not even say goodbye.

A new wave rolled in, and I wanted my mommy. I was again a little girl who believed her mommy would magically make all the pain go away. Squinting at the storm, I knew that the truth was there was no mommy to help me out of this one. After my mom called for the second time, I thought, "Why can't I think about my husband? Do I love him? Will he miss me if I die? Why did I get into mountain climbing?" Why can't I think about my husband? Those questions pushed me back deeper into despair. I didn't have the answers and couldn't think about it.

## Mount Massive

Colorado's 14,421-foot Mount Massive
Photo by John Kirk

One day in June 2003, at my restaurant job, my friend, Sue, asked me, "Hey Alyson, do you want to hike a Fourteener next weekend with me and a group of friends? I go out with this group once a year and we try to get a new Fourteener each time."

I was a Colorado native, but I had to ask, "What's a Fourteener?"

Incredulous, Sue replied, "Alyson, Colorado has 54 mountains over fourteen thousand feet in elevation. Most of these Fourteeners are scattered across the state and require an all-day hike. Fourteeners provide an excellent workout, and you get to enjoy like-minded friends, amazing views, and nature. What do you say?"

"Amazing. That's exactly what I need and want. Count me in. I can't wait."

As the next week sped by, I quivered with excitement. Besides skiing at resorts near Denver, I had never been into the heartland of Colorado's mountains. The Fourteener we were climbing, Mount Massive, was in the center of Colorado's highest mountains. I felt like I could dance to the top.

I had never done anything like this before, so I had no idea what to expect. I packed what Sue told me to bring and showed up at the prescribed meeting place in Denver at 3:30 a.m. Sue explained that we needed to start early to beat the usual afternoon thunderstorms. We had a two-hour drive, then a 14-mile hike with a hefty elevation gain. I was so excited that I couldn't sleep, so the early departure was not a problem. Even in the middle of the night, Sue's friends were passionate and put excitement into the air. I was finally meeting like-minded people who would help me find my mountain legs.

Eight of us arrived at the trailhead at 6:30 a.m., prepared for the hike, hefted our packs and started hiking at 6:45 a.m. Like Echo Lake, the environment I was entering immediately captivated me. Bird chirps filled my ears, the pine trees' scent flooded my nose, water rushing under a bridge told my legs to go faster, and the tree-filtered sunrise captured my eyes. It was intoxicating.

As we hiked, the scenery steadily became more majestic. When we passed treeline and entered the alpine zone, I felt like I had been released from jail. We stopped to breathe the thinning air, eat, drink, and soak in the views. Other peaks popped into view and my eyes darted from summit to higher summit. All my life I had been missing out on amazing experiences like this. What had I been doing?

I was determined to stay at the front of the group and met a fit guy named Travis who easily stayed in front with me. After several hours, we finally saw the summit, and I felt my first rush of summit fever. Travis and I worked hard to be the first two on top. We reached the summit at noon and were a bit amazed that we were a half hour ahead of everyone else.

On the summit, I transcended to become one with Earth. I had been lost my whole life but had finally found my way home. I was simultaneously free, happy, and felt a life purpose. I knew I could be more in touch with my spirituality in the mountains, especially on a high summit. I had been searching for many years, and finally found a rush of answers on Mount Massive. It was life changing. I was home.

The weather was perfect; there was not a cloud in the sky. I gazed at mountains in every direction and watched lakes glisten in the valleys between them. I learned that I was at 14,421 feet and that Massive was the second highest peak in Colorado. Wow! Second highest. Where was the highest? I did not have to look far. Following a finger point, I saw Mount Elbert, Colorado's highest peak, a mere five miles to the south. It looked large but gentle. When could I climb Elbert? We were all one with the mountain that day. Tingling, I sensed that this experience would change me for the rest of my life. I seemed to have found my passion.

## More Fourteeners, Please

After my transcendence on Massive's summit, I wanted more. much more. My life experiences so far had taught me that I had a serious addictive personality. I needed to point my passion in a positive direction. It was early summer, and I had several months in front of me to climb more of Colorado's spectacular Fourteeners.

Back at the Mount Massive trailhead, Travis and I exchanged numbers and chatted excitedly about climbing more Fourteeners together later that summer. Travis told me about a guidebook written by Gerry Roach called Colorado's Fourteeners: From Hikes to Climbs. He said that Gerry's book was the bible for hiking Fourteeners and that I needed my own copy so I could start making plans.

After Massive, I dashed out and bought Gerry's Fourteeners guide. The book wasn't just a guide to the mountains; it was a light shining on my new obsession. I read the book from front to back, and then carefully studied it again. I learned about the different mountain ranges, their many Fourteeners, and a dizzying number of routes. I had no idea that Colorado had so many high peaks to climb. Then, adding in Gerry's extra credits and variations, there were hundreds of adventures waiting for me. Reading Gerry's book was better than discovering a new sport. Gripping the edge of the table, I knew that this was something I would be doing for the rest of my life.

I continued to learn about the difficulty ratings for each route. I quickly realized that Massive was a walk up, but other Fourteeners were more difficult. There were, however, many easy Fourteeners, so I had to choose carefully. I knew that I was a rookie charging into a new sport, and that mountains harbor many dangers —especially for someone climbing alone.

I found two relatively easy Fourteeners in Gerry's book that were only a little over an hour drive from Denver. I learned that 14,270-foot Grays Peak was the highest peak in Colorado's Front Range that I had been looking at in the distance my whole life. Grays' companion peak, Torreys, was only three feet lower, and these were the two highest peaks in the Front Range. I also learned that these are the only Colorado Fourteeners on the Continental Divide.

With my addictive personality already kicking in, I wanted to do Grays and Torreys the next weekend after Massive. Both Sue and Travis were busy, and I didn't want to go alone, so I talked my brother, Kyle, sister Sarah, and Sarah's friend, Megan, into going with me. Talk about the blind leading the blind. They had zero idea about what they were getting themselves into. However, I did have my Massive experience to draw on, and Gerry's guide helped. There is a trail to the top of Grays, so all we had to do was follow the trail.

We launched our little expedition the next weekend. Remembering Sue's lecture about the hazards of afternoon thunderstorms, we started our day early. Megan and I were in better shape than Sarah and Kyle, so we carried all their gear. We had no trouble following the trail and found ourselves prancing on top of Grays before noon. Well, I was prancing. Sarah, Megan, and Kyle had never been to 14,000 feet before and were "sucking wind," as I had learned to call it. Still, they loved the experience. Sitting still on the summit, their pulse dropped below wind-sucking status, and we enjoyed the expanse of surrounding summits. Denver was too far away to matter, and we faced west, looking for more adventures. For me, I discovered another new feeling of bonding with my sister and brother. After the big pull up Grays, we found the traverse over to Torreys to be much easier. Sparks of inspiration were firing in my brain. Two peaks for the price of one hike.

I was hooked. I had ignited a peak-bagging bonfire in my soul. Better, my damaging addictions had morphed into pure motivation. All I had to do was stay on my new path.

Travis and I made climbing plans for several weekends in July, and our next adventure was a group of four Fourteeners that were all connected by a rolling ridge. Our four Fourteeners were Mounts Lincoln, Democrat, Bross, and Cameron. The highest of the four was 14,286-foot Mount Lincoln, and Gerry's book quickly told me that Lincoln was the highest peak in the Tenmile-Mosquito Range, the next major range west of the Front Range. Lincoln was also higher than Grays. Upwards and outwards. Pure progress. This sounded like the perfect adventure.

I began to feel joy in my new path. Up early, drive and chat with my companion, and hit the trail at sunrise. Travis and I did Gerry's famous "Decalibron" combination route to hit all four peaks. We started with shapely Democrat, ran the ridge to the unofficial peak Cameron, then perched on the highest, Lincoln. The air at 14,000 feet felt normal now, and my legs twitched for more action. I didn't have to wait long. We completed our ramble with the easy traverse over to Bross. Four peaks for the price of one hike.

On the rounded summit of Bross, Travis and I met another group of hikers. They were all bubbling with summit energy, and I came to understand that mountaineers are always free.

After a round of summit photos, Travis and I hiked down with the other group, and I chatted with a girl named Jordan. We clicked right away, since Jordan was serious about hiking Fourteeners, and she was also a marathon runner. Back at the trailhead, we exchanged numbers and made plans to get out together soon.

Back home, I felt great. I now had seven Fourteeners under my belt and a growing list of friends to climb with. My coughing was a dim memory.

# Dry Drunks

I had one problem that almost everybody will recognize. After losing my decent real estate job and taking the low-paying restaurant job, I was having trouble with money. I was trying to mend my relationship with my parents and asked them if I could move in with them again until I got a new real estate job. They both said fine, so I moved back into my old memory-ridden family home after a multi-year absence. I thought that things would be completely different since my father had quit drinking to save his marriage, and I had found my new life. Of course, it would not be so simple.

Things were somewhat different, but the fighting between my parents was still there. Their fighting was worse than normal married couple bickering. My father had indeed stopped drinking, but he kept most of his emotionally abusive behaviors. He was a textbook example of a dry drunk. He seemed to have a handle on his physical violence, mainly punching holes in the walls and breaking things, but I was still dealing with the same person.

With my list of climbs growing, I wanted to share my adventures and new passion with my family. However, when I came home from a wonderful weekend of climbing, I would only get a few sentences into my description before my father would interrupt with mean responses. He thought my new energized life was a step backwards. He never wanted to hear anything about mountains. He thought climbing was stupid and dangerous. My inner voice, still fueled by my vows, thought it was the other way around. It crawled back into my consciousness that my father was an oblivious dream-crusher.

My mom acted interested in the beginning, but soon grew sick of my stories. I measured the decline by counting down how many sentences I could get into my explanations before I was interrupted with the mundane. When nobody could handle even one sentence, I shut up and held my memories in my special place. I had the same problem with my older brother, Jason. He now had two kids and I think he couldn't stand to hear about the fun things I was doing. More than that, I always felt like he thought I needed to have a family and "grow up." Jason could only echo my father's sentiments.

It was a deep pang that most of my family never wanted to hear about my passion. My sister Sarah cared, since she had her own passions with mountains and running. She was the only one. I grew to understand that the rest of my family didn't want to hear about deep motivations, since none of them had their own fire. They simply had no basis for understanding.

## Jordan

Jordan was my age and lived in Colorado Springs, a 45-minute drive from my house. Jordan was easier to be with than Sue who was 15 years older than me. I found more similarities with Jordan, and we would be inseparable for the next year. For the rest of the 2003 summer, we hiked Fourteeners together, and it was wonderful to have a partner who enjoyed the peaks as much as I did. Beyond the guidebook lessons, we both learned first-hand that some Fourteeners were tough. I also learned that many people only did a few Fourteeners each summer and devoted their life to finishing them all. I reasoned that, since there are only 54 Fourteeners, I didn't want to spend my whole life climbing them. I wanted to gobble them all now, then do other mountains.

## Josh and JB

In late August, Jordan and I decided to climb Mounts Belford and Oxford. Because of valley vagaries, the easiest way to do both peaks is to hike up Belford, traverse to Oxford, then climb back to a point close to the Belford's summit before descending back to the original trailhead. Colder air was already fingering the heights and there was a little snow on the peaks, but that was not going to stop us. The re-climb of Belford would make this effort one of our longest adventures.

After our patented early start, Belford and Oxford's summits flowed under our feet. Back near Belford's summit, a young black lab ran to us, jumped, sniffed, and licked us profusely. He was adorable, and I fell in love immediately. A moment later, his owner approached and apologized for his dog's overzealous greeting. We did not mind and introduced ourselves. The dog's owner was Josh and his dog was simply JB. We decided to hike back to our car with Josh and JB.

My first impression of Josh was that he was kind, had dynamic blue eyes, and owned an amazing dog. However, he was shorter than me, and I never dated guys shorter than me. After hiking back to the car with Josh and learning a lot about him, I figured he would be a good climbing partner in the future. He didn't live far from me and was also trying to climb all the Fourteeners. Back at the trailhead, Josh and I exchanged email addresses and promises for getting together for more peak climbs. Jordan did not like Josh at all, and I didn't understand why. I would find out later.

Josh emailed me a couple of days later, and we planned our next Fourteener climb, Mount Shavano, in two weeks. All my juices were still flowing and my newfound passion was intense. Josh, JB, and I really enjoyed each other's company on Shavano, and got to know each other better. Josh was eight years older than me and quite successful. I couldn't remember the last time I had a male friend who was sober, smart, and going somewhere with their life. Suddenly, I felt blessed to never have ended up pregnant with one of the losers I was dating when I was into drinking and drugs.

After Shavano, Josh and I wanted to plan more Fourteeners but winter injected itself, so we started doing other activities together. Josh was good looking, but he wasn't exactly my type and, darn, he was shorter than me. Nevertheless, Josh's kind-heartedness grew on me. Like a vine slowly crawling up a wall, I felt my feelings for Josh growing. He was unique in my life, athletic, successful, and motivated to better himself. Love? I didn't know about that yet, but I reasoned that being around Josh would be a good choice on my new life path. Josh and I spent the next year hiking, climbing, skiing, and traveling, and even indulged in controlled drinking and partying. We had fun in a balanced manner. During this time, Jordan and I drifted apart. She still didn't like Josh, and now she liked him even less because he took me away from our friendship.

It took me a while to introduce Josh to my family. I was nervous about bringing him home because I never knew what to expect from my father. In the beginning, Josh clicked with most of my family because he was a drinker like everyone in my family. Big family gatherings always involved alcohol and everyone sloshed their way to a good time.

Later, my family was surprised by Josh. No one thought he was my type and my father did not like him, but liked Josh's dog, JB, a lot more than he liked me. JB and I were bonded. I would run, walk, and hike with him and he was my number one partner for anything I did.

## Marathon

Josh and I had dated for a year when I decided to run my first full marathon. I was at my healthy high school weight and had done several half marathons, so I felt ready for the challenge. I was nervous looking for which marathon to run, since I knew it had to have beautiful surroundings and views. I loved running for the pure joy of the air, the scenery, and the exercise. I finally found the Durango Marathon on October 9, 2005. I had never been to Durango in southwest Colorado, but Josh told me I would love it. He said it was a six-hour drive through the heart of Colorado's mountains and that I would run through fall colors surrounded by views and peaks. I was sold and immediately signed up for the race.

When the time arrived, Josh and I drove to Durango. On our transit, we went through spectacular places that I had never seen and didn't even know existed. Between the surrounding peaks and pre-race jitters, my adrenaline was working overtime. I was also strangely full of joy.

Like my first half marathon, my first marathon was a transcending experience. We launched from the Fort Lewis College campus where kind people were supporting me. As I had secretly feared, the marathon was hard. We were at high altitude where I wasn't used to running, it was windy, and combined with the reality of 26.2 miles, I felt some of my joy dissipate. As predicted in many running books, I hit the wall between miles 17-20 and, for a bit, I didn't know if I could make it. I pretended I was on top of a mountain and still had to descend. There was no quit option there, and there would be no quit today either. Digging deeper than I had in any of my half marathons, I persevered to reach the finish line in downtown Durango with a time of 4:01:46.

Right after I finished, another runner's high made me feel better than any drug or drink could have. I experienced a feeling of well-being and tingled with joy. The rush matched how I felt on top of Mount Massive. With hard work, determination, training, then gutting it out late in the race, I had finished my first marathon.

On the drive home I was so excited that I called home to tell my mom about my accomplishment. I wavered when my father answered, but launched into my excited explanation. I told him that I got second place in my age group. Not bad for a rookie, eh? Then, my father spoke the unspeakable. "That's all? Why didn't you get first?" He didn't congratulate me, he wasn't happy or excited, and I hung up on him in tears. Why? What did he get out of it? There was no rational explanation. Perhaps he was angry with himself and what his life had become. Why take it out on us? He can be such a mean man. He hurts my heart. He has no idea what emotional pain he causes me. Why can't he be proud of me?

I wallowed in self-pity, thinking that all I had done was disappoint my father.

*Even if I survive, he would never say he loved me or that he's happy that I'm okay. He'll say, "I told you so." Worse, he will pontificate that climbing mountains is dangerous and a waste of time. I should stop hiking, have kids, be like mom, and become "normal." Huh? My mom lived in hell. The hell with that. I don't want to be "normal."*

I jerked hard enough that Prakash reached for my shoulders. My spastic movement reinvigorated the pain. I was still on the side of a mountain, now in the dark, in February, in a snowstorm, and I was still dying.

Prakash made another call to SAR and was put on hold while they radioed the teams for an update. He stood in front of me to block the wind and held me with his left arm. He put his ski helmet on to keep warm. Rime ice began to coat his glasses, right eyebrow, and eyelashes. After ten minutes, the call simply dropped. Frustrated, Prakash headed uphill to search for a better phone signal.

*It's too late. I've been here all day watching my life flash before me.* I wondered, *I don't know why I'm not concerned about what my death would do to my husband, or why I don't feel the need or desire for him to be with me, or why I have no need to say goodbye, or even that I loved him.*

I was beyond tired and cold. My thoughts still had me, but I did not have my body. With what I had left, I tried to think about all the peaks I had left to climb, all the races left to run, love to share, and the many experiences left to be relished. A small smile crept across my face as the darkness pulled its blanket tight around me.

# Chapter 10 – Obsession

The march of minutes to my inevitable death was steady and unstoppable. I had been locked in the same position for over ten hours. I was frozen. I was falling into despair and hopelessness. With each tick, my chances for survival decreased. We both knew that finding me in the middle of the night in a howling whiteout was going to be difficult and perhaps impossible. We could scream at the top of our lungs, but the wind would easily extinguish our sound. Prakash thought that if he could head down into the trees, he might be able to find the rescue team and lead them back to me. However, the trees and the trail were more than a mile away. Even after relaying GPS coordinates, I still felt like a snowflake in a blizzard.

Having Prakash with me sacrificing everything to save my life made me feel guilty for thinking that I might quit. Still, it would be so easy to die. I was now alone. All I had to do was close my eyes and drift away. Let my father live in his inferno of negativity. Let him feel guilt. No. I had to think of something positive. Something positive. *Positive.*

## Jim and Cappy

During my time as a waitress, I developed friendships with my regular customers. When they came to the restaurant, they would ask to sit in my section. One couple, in particular, was Jim and Cappy who were in their late sixties. Both had served in the Army and that's how they met. Jim and Cappy saw me at the restaurant once a week. After a year of waiting on them as customers, we had developed a good friendship. They always provided a positive, supportive example.

Eventually, I told them about my family and my past. They were compassionate and understanding about how difficult it was to overcome my family issues. Jim and Cappy were the best people I associated with in the restaurant, and the only decent friendship I had there. Friendship and role models come in all shapes, sizes, and ages. I felt blessed to have met these wonderful people.

Alyson with Jim and Cappy

## Boston Marathon

After my first marathon, I wasn't smitten—I was in love. My obsessive-compulsive personality screamed at me to do more marathons and do them now. After the Durango Marathon, I set my sights on the Rock 'n' Roll Arizona Marathon in Phoenix on Jan 15, 2006. Living and training in Denver at over 5,000 feet gave me an advantage, and running a marathon in Phoenix at 1,200 feet should help me. I wondered if running at a much lower elevation would increase my leg speed, endurance, or both. Would my lungs drive my feet faster than they could handle? Would I trip? Nah. For the next three months, I got into the best shape of my life. I worked hard on my diet and got my weight right where I wanted it.

I ran the Rock 'n' Roll Marathon in 3:38:30, taking 23 minutes off my previous time. More important, I qualified for the Boston Marathon by beating their qualifying time of 3:40. My spirit soared. This was only my second marathon, and I was now going to run the Super Bowl of marathons. I signed up for the Boston

Marathon to be held on April 16, 2007. I had a year to train and lose more weight.

Traveling to the east coast was a first for me. I had not traveled much as a child, and certainly never to Boston. I was like a kid lost in an amusement park. A few years earlier, I was a hundred pounds heavier, an alcoholic, a drug user, and a pack-a-day smoker. I felt so proud of the person I was becoming.

Ever since I worked at the restaurant, Jim and Cappy had been two of my best friends. They had no children of their own and had treated me as their surrogate child. They greatly helped me get through my hard times, and I grew to love them like the parents I never had. Josh and I planned to meet Jim and Cappy in Boston, and stay with them at Cappy's brother's house. At this point, Josh and I had been dating for a while, and Josh was one of my biggest supporters. Now, adding Jim and Cappy's support, it all seemed like a super-sized dream.

People propose, but nature can easily dispose. A day before the race, we were informed that the mighty Boston Marathon might be canceled because a nor'easter was blasting the entire area. I had no idea what a nor'easter was but quickly learned that these storms can bring hurricane-force winds and blizzard conditions. This storm looked like snow, not rain. The Boston Marathon is a marquee sporting event for all of America. Could it, would it be canceled? I and thousands of other runners were poised.

I was plagued with devastating thoughts. Even if the race wasn't canceled, would I be able to run through this storm for 26.2 miles? I was now skinny, had little body fat, and got cold easily. While Josh and I were in our pre-race hotel room preparing, I went digging through my suitcase looking for warm clothing. I found a letter with my name on it.

I opened the letter and found a good luck card. My mom, sister, and two younger brothers had all wished me luck and signed the card. They also said how proud they were of me. Reading this card brought tears to my eyes. They were not good at expressing these things verbally, and their words warmed my heart. I knew that no matter how bad it became during the race, it could always be worse, and I had the determination to persevere through anything. I went to bed the night before the marathon still not knowing if I would race, but that I would win in the lifelong run.

The race officials made their decision in the night and decided not to cancel the race. I woke to flip my emotions again. Yikes. In motion toward the starting line, there was only one emotion: race. Boston has 20,000 runners; ten times more than I had ever been with for any event. Thousands more lined the streets to cheer the runners. Boom. We were off on the famous journey called the Boston Marathon.

The weather was adverse but not impossible and, since everybody was enduring the same conditions, we all felt an embracing companionship. Finally running, my mind settled, and I could focus on the basics: stride, form, pace, breath, the next turn, and the next hill.

Running long distances became an obsession, and I looked forward to the runner's high that I found late in the race. Probably an old survival instinct, my brain released feel-good chemicals to mask running's discomforts. I could float along. This high had replaced the alleged highs that I sought with alcohol and drugs. My old highs always ended up being lows. *The heck with them.* I knew my personality would seek an addiction and that running was vastly better than my earlier wallowing.

I maintained form, didn't bonk, and finished the Boston Marathon with a time of 3:29:55, my fastest time yet. Josh, Jim, and Cappy found me in the crush of people at the finish, hugged, and congratulated me. It was obvious that they were proud of me, and it was a pivotal moment for me. Of course, I was proud, but even more, all-embracing. I loved running, and felt that all things were possible.

## Bachelor's Degree

My dad had spent years telling me college was a waste of time and money. However, after struggling in the real estate business and working in restaurants, I was tired of staring at the small paychecks and counting the pennies in my tips wondering how I could manage on that measly amount. My lack of a degree felt like a void. Also, I now had the example of Josh who had a degree and a good job. If I wanted more opportunities, I had to get a college degree.

So, again, I tossed my father's advice into my mental trash can and stuck with what I knew was right for me. I wasn't one of those people who was ready for college right after high school. That would have been a waste of money. I knew in my gut when I was ready. Waiting tables and visualizing the rest of my life as a waitress gave me the drive to want more. I knew I needed to go to college so I started researching where I wanted to go, how much it was going to cost, and what I wanted to be when I grew up. Before long, I was applying for student loans and enrolled in classes at Metro State. It was my start to a better life. I started at Metro State then transferred to CU Denver to finish both my bachelor's and master's degrees there.

Over these years, I took out several student loans, which bothered me, but definitely made me work harder for my education. Since it was my decision, money, and time, I focused my effort like the degree was a finish line or mountain summit. Josh encouraged me as well and thought school was a good idea for me. In contrast to my father's venom, it was wonderful to have someone supporting me. It made my hard decision a no-brainer.

While the decision was easy, getting the degree was tough. I briefly worked as a personal assistant for Sandy and Jerry Weigand. After they heard my story, the Weigands helped me financially, and I'm not sure that I would have finished without their help. I spent several years getting my bachelor's degree in business management, graduating on December 15, 2007. My parents came to my graduation and, for once, I felt that maybe my father was a little bit proud of me. I finished that year feeling positive about my future. I was in shape, running, climbing, and my weight was under control. What could go wrong?

# ED

One day, while my friend Jordan and I were doing a 20-mile training run, she told me about her roommate's eating disorders. I had never heard much about eating disorders and was curious. Jordan explained anorexia and bulimia, and told me that one of her roommates was anorexic and one was bulimic. She told me how much it upset her that the bulimic roommate would eat most of the food in their house, then throw it up. This sounded absurd to me. Why would someone do that? What a waste of money. I knew about getting fat, but this was the first time I had heard about the opposite extreme. Jordan went on to explain that more people than we know suffer from eating disorders. I had no idea of the twisted turn my life would soon take.

After the Boston Marathon, I was obsessed with running. At that point, I was already skinny. I ate almost no fat or sugar, only sugar substitutes. I had figured out that the lighter I was, the faster my times would be. A few years earlier my weight was over 220 pounds, and I was now approaching 120 pounds. At first, the compliments I received were flattering. People who knew me when I was fat then watched me transform my body into a healthier figure were encouraging to me. However, those compliments stopped when I took my weight loss to an unhealthy level. At one point, you could see my chest bones, and my veins popped out of my arms. Over time, I became afraid of food. I was scared to eat because I didn't want to gain weight and be fat again. I trained hard for running, and I also hiked all the time. That was my new life, and I felt that I was honoring it but I was unhealthy again.

Alyson - too skinny?

Josh and I were working on climbing all of Colorado's Fourteeners. Josh had about 20 more than I did so, to catch up with him, I went out with JB to do the peaks he had already done. I loved being alone in the mountains, working hard all day, then being rewarded with stunning views and an abiding sense of achievement on a summit. There was nothing else quite like it. However, with my running and hiking combined, I was only eating a fraction of the calories that I needed for the activity I was doing. My weight continued to drop.

When I reached 115 pounds, I started dreaming about food. My dreams were about the foods that I was convinced were forbidden. I would dream of cakes, donuts, cookies, candy, bread, fast food, brownies, and even popcorn. I chewed sugar-free gum to keep from stuffing other foods in my mouth. When my dreams occurred on a regular basis, I remembered Jordan and her roommates' eating disorders. I thought about how easy it would be to eat all my dream foods, then throw them up. I reasoned that I wouldn't gain weight, but I could live my dream. By any rational standard, this thinking was messed up, but I was not rational. What I didn't understand was that my brain was not getting proper nutrients, and that led to my illogical thinking. I was on the brink of another downward spiral.

The first time I ever engaged in bulimia was after my little brother's high school graduation. He had a huge cake at his party that was only half eaten. I was house sitting, and my mom asked if I would take the cake over to my friend's house for them to have when they returned. I was fine with that, and took the cake back to the house with me.

That evening I was alone watching a movie, and the thought of the cake in the other room consumed my thinking. I thought, "Okay, just one piece." I got up and followed my feet to the cake. I stared at it for a suspended moment then, reasoning that calories consumed standing up don't count, I ate a thin slice. Delicious. Now one more. I sat down and gobbled the entire cake. Since my stomach had shrunk from my starving, I was so full by the time I was done that I had to throw it up. I went to the bathroom, stuck my fingers down my throat, and out it came. Out, out, out! I was now downward bound, but nobody saw me do it.

After my first experience with bulimia, all the foods I would never dare allow myself to eat came to the forefront of my thinking. I could now eat and throw up afterward. My brain ran amok on me, and these thoughts consumed me all day long. I was still in touch enough to be embarrassed, so I was super secretive about my disorder. I covered my tracks so no one would find out. I knew that what I was doing was wrong, wrong, wrong, but my addictive personality took over, and I slithered down my slippery slope.

When I was obviously anorexic, my mom sat me down for a talk. She said that I looked disgusting and needed to gain weight. She told me I needed to get help and to go see a doctor. Those were good mom things to say, and they were true, but I was not rational. Her talk made me angry. My family discussions had never gone well in the past, so I fell into my old pattern of resentment. My mom's words hurt me, but deep down I knew she was right. Later, I agreed to go to a doctor and to see a nutritionist.

The nutritionist I went to thought I was a complete joke. First, she had to know how much I exercised to compute how much I should be eating. When I told her about my exercise program, she was blown away. Flabbergasted, she told me that I needed rest days and that I needed to cut my exercise program in half. She made some valid points, but didn't understand what it takes to train for marathons and mountain climbing. She was also fat. How can a nutritionist be fat? Doesn't it go against their job description? I'm sure she didn't exercise either, so she had no idea what she was talking about. I never saw her again.

My mom kept after me and that eroded our relationship. She was fond of saying, "Eat a hamburger Alyson, it's not going to kill you." One of the primary tenants of my new life program was that I would choose my directions and means. I had spent years kowtowing to other's ideas about what I should do and who I should be. I was done with that.

I was steady with my running and hiking program, but my eating disorder got worse. The other big event was my relationship with Josh. I really wasn't dating Josh. I felt like I was dating my eating disorder and using Josh as a cover so that no one would know. It became so bad that I believed I could live with my eating disorder for the rest of my life, and no one would ever know. I could be skinny and sexy forever and eat the bad stuff. I was convinced that there was nothing wrong with my train of thought, or how I lived. Everything was backwards in my mind. The reality was that I was sliding deeper into my relationship with Josh, but my heart knew that he was not a soul-mate. Josh was a great guy and he helped me more than I could have hoped for, but he felt like a roommate, not a life mate or a soul-mate.

## Fantastic Fourteeners

As the summer of 2008 rolled along, I kept climbing Fourteeners. Josh and I had signed up for the website 14ers.com, and we made new friends there for group hikes up Fourteeners. I met a woman named Caroline who became a good hiking partner. Caroline and I had the same goal, and decided to finish the Fourteeners together.

I was outside year-round climbing Fourteeners or doing trail runs. Since I went out every weekend, I passed Josh and started doing Fourteeners that Josh hadn't done. Josh wasn't as driven as I was.

By August, Josh, who was spending most of his time biking, still had several more to go, but I was down to my last one. My friend Caroline and I planned our Fourteener finish together on 14,130-foot Capitol Peak, which many climbers consider to be Colorado's hardest Fourteener. Capitol requires a 6.2-mile approach hike up to Capitol Lake nestled below Capitol's huge north face. You have to traverse Capitol's notorious knife-edge ridge, where you can peer down a thousand feet on either side of the ridge. Beyond the knife-edge, the remaining route to the summit is convoluted and often exposed, where a fall would be fatal.

Capitol has it all, and was a stunning final Fourteener for us. We had a group of eight along for our finishing climb, including my little brother, Daniel, who loved Capitol's more technical sections. It was wonderful to have him along to share the experience and joy of my goal completion. On the exposed summit, we discovered that a friend carried up a bottle of champagne for a grand toast to our quest. Fortunately, when we divided the bottle into eight glasses, there wasn't enough bubbly for anyone to get smashed, but it was a toast to remember.

Alyson's Capitol Fourteener Finish

It had taken me a little over five years to climb Colorado's Fourteeners. This was far from a speed record, but I had been dealing with other life mountains during that time. I was surprised at the feelings of accomplishment that washed over me. My marathons had lasted a few hours, but this five-year project filled me with a joy that had not touched me before. It deepened my resolve to create a better-balanced life.

Caroline and I were ecstatic with our achievement, and decided to throw a party at the house I shared with Josh the following weekend with our friends and family. The guest list for our extravagant Fourteener finisher party grew as Caroline and I exchanged wild winks. I still drank in what I had proclaimed to be moderation. I had my eating disorder now, so I didn't need to drink to excess. It would only be consuming empty calories that would make me fat. I certainly wouldn't drink and drive.

We decided to get a keg of beer for our party and many other booze bottles appeared on the table. It was time to celebrate with our friends. Lucifer arrived and, after I started drinking, I couldn't stop. I was throwing up by seven p.m. That evening, almost everyone there got drunk, and this night ended up changing my life.

I stepped outside of my drunken self and saw myself and everyone else. I was supposed to be celebrating a big accomplishment, and I wouldn't even remember it. I watched myself doing this for the rest of my life. Then I saw that I was becoming my father. That did it, and I flipped a switch in my addled but still functional brain. I was sick and tired of thinking that booze had to be involved in celebration. I barfed one more time to get what remained out, and that was it. I would never take another drink.

Late that night, I vowed in front of Josh, my family, and friends, that I would never take another drink. I vowed that I was done drinking for the rest of my life. Of course, no one believed me, since I had been a raging alcoholic for years. Yes, I calmed down, but nobody saw me giving it up for good. I liked that people didn't think I could do it, because that further empowered me to do it. I love when people tell me that I can't do something. Then, it's a guarantee that I will do it.

Mom, Kyle, Sarah, Daniel, Alyson, Jason, Dad

## Manias

I ran as many marathons as I could sign up for. My thoughts switched to the next scheduled race after finishing a marathon. I was signed up for more than one race at a time. My dresser was filling up with marathon tee-shirts. If a non-runner asked me about my racing, I spoke with such passion that the questioner regretted asking and walked away. I started to think of a marathon as a training run. I was an addict, and a proud one.

I joined a club called Marathon Maniacs, touted as the world's most insane running club, where they advertised nine levels of marathon insanity. They freely used the word insane. I met other obsessive people like me, which helped me feel normal. I trumpeted a new mantra, "What is mania for some is normal for others." I had not yet learned the differences between insanity, obsession, and motivation, or what any of this might mean for me in the long run. For now, run was the operative word, and the longer, the better.

Over time, Josh didn't want to climb with me. We had been together for several years now, and I don't think he was interested in trying to impress me anymore. He told me he was burned out on getting up early to go hiking. Josh wanted to get up late and go mountain biking or dirt biking. He told me that after he finished the Fourteeners, he was going to do other activities. That broke my heart because I hated mountain biking and dirt biking. I wanted nothing to do with either.

After I finished the Fourteeners, I wanted to climb other mountains. I wanted a life of climbing as many peaks as I could. Without Josh, I saw myself being alone. This made me sad because I thought I would have a soul-mate to run around and climb mountains with me. I wanted someone who was as obsessive as me and wanted to climb everything. Now, this person that I met on the summit of a Fourteener told me he was done climbing and wanted to ride around on a dirt bike. I could not do that. I also would not be subservient like my mom and stick with a bad situation. Josh and I had changed over time and, in my heart, I knew that it did not make sense to stay together.

Josh was a hard-working, kindhearted person. In the beginning I thought I was in love with him, but I knew it wasn't the kind of love I was looking for with a lifelong soul-mate. However, Josh was the first person who treated me well and inspired me to be better, and I loved him for that. I grew to love Josh as a good friend, not a life-mate. To ease my conflict, I found the next cake.

As my eating disorder worsened, I knew I needed help. My brain chemistry was way off, and my binge thoughts consumed me. When I was semi-rational, I knew my long-term health was being jeopardized. I also grew to realize that bulimia could kill me. For the first few years, I thought that no one ever had to know and I could live with it forever, but then I reached a point where I wanted to die. The thought of living with this awful eating disorder for the rest of my life made me not want to live anymore. I was trapped in a triple jeopardy. I couldn't be with Josh and my heart was in two pieces. I couldn't break out of bulimia, so I wanted to die. I knew bulimia would eventually kill me, probably sooner than later. My disorder was more powerful than my addiction to drinking, drugs, and smoking had been. I had quit all three of those things. They were not easy to quit. Each one was actually quite hard, but with the right life style changes, motivation and willingness I did it! The difference here was I didn't need drinking, drugs, or smoking to live. I did need food. This was a different kind of battle. A battle I did not know if I could win.

In desperation, I opened up to Josh about my disorder. I was embarrassed and ashamed, and it was almost impossible to tell him about it. To my amazement and relief, Josh was supportive and normal. I was sure that he would think I was crazy. His support at my lowest point probably saved my life. I think he and everyone else knew that I had an eating disorder, but no one said anything.

My mom had been telling me that I needed to gain weight, but that was about it. With support from Josh, I opened up to my parents as well. I explained to them that I had both anorexia and bulimia. My mom said that she knew I was anorexic, but the bulimia took everyone by surprise. No one understood how I could stuff my face then throw up. I tried to explain it further, but that led to frustration, and I dove back into silence. No one I opened up to about my problems with eating could really understand what I was going through. I felt more trapped than ever.

I began therapy with Josh and my parents to discuss my disorder, and found an eating disorder specialist to help me as well. I started attending sessions at an eating disorder support group called Food Addicts Anonymous, or FAA, to tell my story and listen to other people's stories. I tried hard to get help, but nothing seemed to work. The stories at FAA were stories; there was no solution. Nothing made the eating disorder, or ED, voice in my head go away. There were times when it would be quiet for a while, but my devil always snuck up on me and became the loudest thing in my brain.

I had always had something to numb the world's pain. Now, my eating disorder became the way I coped with life. Instead of drinking and drugs, I used bulimia to deal with my emotions and frustrations. The professional help I sought had not helped.

After years, one of my therapists said I needed to have a bone density scan to see what my eating disorder was doing to my bones. I had the scan. I wouldn't have believed the results if I had not seen it with my own eyes. How could a young, athletic, marathon-running, mountain-climbing woman have the bones of a 60-year-old person?

After seeing the bone density scan results, I knew I had to stop talking about myself in the third person. The test and the sight of me essentially dead jolted me back to reality. I realized that any day, I would no longer be able to run or climb. I wanted to live a long life enjoying my passions and for that I needed healthy bones. I had my first desire to reverse my disorder. I knew that if it was to be, it was up to me. I knew that I was way behind the curve, and that bulimia could still kill me. My addictive personality flipped over to solving my problem. I just hoped that it wasn't too late.

## Now What?

After my Fourteener finish and marathon successes, I had to face the rest of my life. I wanted to go on to climb other peaks, but all my climbing partners had other goals. Many of them wanted to pursue "The Grid," where you try to climb every Fourteener in every season or—gasp—in every calendar month. That meant climbing the Fourteeners over and over, and in winter. I didn't want to repeat the same peaks; I wanted to explore new summits. I had seen enough from the Fourteener summits to know there are hundreds of other Colorado peaks that few people visit, and I felt their siren call.

Outside my circle of climbing friends, everyone else thought the Fourteeners were a phase for me. They assumed I would now get married and have kids. Josh asked me if I would now go biking with him. I didn't want to do that because I loved running and hiking. I had been with Josh for four years, and our families kept pressuring us to get married and have kids. I told my family that I didn't want to have children. The thought of having my own kids right now made me feel sick. Family and societal pressures only increased my feelings. I knew that having children right now would be life changing and bad for me.

Deep inside, I knew that one reason I didn't want kids was because I was with Josh and he was not the man I was meant to spend the rest of my life with. Another reason was the fact that, for most of my childhood, I had to help raise my brothers and sister. I worked in a mothering role then, and had lost much of my own childhood. With gathering resentment, I now felt that my childhood had been taken from me. I was determined to hang on to the rest of my life.

Josh and I now did separate activities on the weekends and saw less and less of each other. I became lonely for attention and love, and used my eating disorder to survive emotional turmoil. It was tough because Josh and his family had done so much for me and had helped me to become a better person. I felt like I owed Josh, but was I supposed to sacrifice my life to pay him back? That made no sense. It didn't feel right with Josh. I had to break free. It's easy to think and say that, but I had no idea how tangled I was in my complex web.

Memories were one thing, but my current reality was something else. My coffin-like slab, the wild wind, the darkness, and the swirling snow were still my truth. My butt was numb, so I tried to move a little to find a better position. Ow! Yes, stinging pain was still with me. I wondered if I would live or die.

I looked over to check on JB, who remained curled tight in a hole he had dug a few feet from me. Snow covered him. Was JB dead? I was not sure how he could still be alive. Reflexively, I reached for him, but my pain shut the motion down. I could not reach him. I tried to shout for JB, and was amazed by what little voice I had left. The wind snatched my pitiful cry. If JB died, it would be my fault, and my already tortured heart twisted into a tornado. JB was my boy, my constant companion, and he had given me unconditional love, about the only love I knew. JB felt like my child, and he could die because he would not leave his mommy. I tried to bring a tear to my eye, but couldn't even do that. Prakash had been gone for what seemed like hours. It was JB and me, and I didn't know about JB. Frozen, racked by pain, and tormented, I was beyond alone. The wind was deafening. The cold was bitter and biting. The pain was unbearable. Being alone with only my tortured thoughts was hell.

My position on the slab of cold rock made my body ache, but I didn't have energy to rearrange my body. The slab's cold harshness thrust tough truths at me. My inability to live authentically had driven my earlier addictions including the eating disorder. My eating disorder had wrecked my bones, and that led to the easy break and my current disaster. If I died on this slab or during the rescue, it would be due to my excesses, and they were due to my inability to accept my authentic self. I could make vows all night about what I would do differently if I survived but, right now, authentic or not, Alyson was dying on this slab.

# Chapter 11 – Living A Lie

I had a group of solid hiking friends from the website 14ers.com and was expanding my horizons beyond the Fourteeners. I discovered another guidebook called Colorado's Lost Creek Wilderness: Classic Summit Hikes to an area southwest of Denver. In the book, the author, Gerry Roach, stated, "If you have climbed all of Colorado's Fourteeners but have never ascended Bison, make it your next outing." That was more than enough motivation for me, and I joined a group heading for 12,431-foot Bison Peak, the highest summit in the Tarryall Mountains and the Lost Creek Wilderness Area.

12,431-foot Bison Peak in Colorado's Lost Creek Wilderness
Photo by John Kirk

The hike up Bison Peak was spectacular. Since it wasn't a Fourteener, I expected a short hike, but was surprised when the climb turned out to be a bit hefty. After steeply hiking up through trees, we passed treeline and reached a flat area called Bison Arm.

Ambling toward the summit, we passed amazing rock formations, and I wondered if I was still in Colorado. The summit was an imposing jumble of rocks, but we found an easy way to scamper up the backside. The peak, the granite formations, the vistas, and the companionship blew me away, and gazing from Bison's summit, I knew that Colorado held hundreds if not thousands of peaks for me to climb. I wanted them all.

On the Bison hike, I clicked with a guy named Shawn, and he became a good hiking buddy. Shawn loved hiking throughout the year and sought out peaks of all elevations. Shawn introduced me to different ranges, and pulled me away from hiking the Fourteeners. While I repeated enjoyable peaks, I also loved finding new adventures. I felt excited and even overwhelmed to learn about how many new Colorado peaks I had to climb. I had Shawn over to the house to meet Josh, so he could approve of Shawn as one of my main hiking partners.

Of course, I told Josh all about the Bison Peak hike, and that I wanted to go back and do the hike again with him. Josh agreed, and we planned on doing the peak again the following weekend. It was early November 2009, the leaves were changing, and the air was crisp. Fall in the Rockies is spectacular. At the trailhead, the weather was less than perfect. We didn't let that discourage us, and charged up the trail.

We reached the summit after four hours, but the weather was now difficult with wind and blowing snow. We retreated from the summit rocks and found a sheltered spot on the lee side so we could enjoy each other's company for a few moments and power up with food and water. I took off my pack and grabbed an apple. Catching me by surprise, Josh got down on one knee and asked me to marry him.

My heart stopped. I was shocked. I was not expecting him to propose and felt off balance. I didn't know what to do with the apple, but stopped rubbing it on my pant leg. Many parts of me were happy and excited, but the many unresolved feelings in my heart kept me from enjoying what was supposed to be a joyful moment.

Josh and I had now been together for five years and were getting pressured from family and friends to get married. Outsiders assumed that we needed to be married, but they did not know my heart. I knew my relationship with Josh wasn't right, but didn't know how to end it. I was comfortable with Josh, but knew that he was not my one true love. Leaving would be hard; there would be pain and discomfort involved. Change is never easy that's why it's easy to stay put to avoid the unknown.

Josh was a good person and treated me well. I could marry him and remain comfortable but, for me, I wanted a soul-mate. I wanted and needed to marry someone who had the same crazy passions I had. I had to control my addictions to bad substances and behaviors, but I also knew my addictions would morph to other obsessive-compulsive passions. It appeared that I now had OCD about mountains. My thoughts consumed me on a daily basis. I reasoned that my dream soul-mate was a fantasy and, even if that person existed, my chances of finding him were slim to none. So, marrying Josh and having a comfortable life was hard to pass up. Was I brave enough to launch a drastic leap into a fantasy that could become a void?

Josh and I had been through a lot together, I did care about him and his family, and the thought of hurting him pained me. Josh and I had fallen for each other when we had the same passions, but had grown apart in our five years together. Before meeting me, Josh had been in numerous long-term relationships, but I had been in none. I think that Josh had never loved his past girlfriends as much as he loved me, so he probably assumed that what we had was as good as it gets. We were balancing on a slippery slope of fate. I knew that settling for less than my soul-mate would catch up with me. With my passionate, over-the-top personality, balanced, quiet, conservative Josh was not the one for me, but I said yes to his proposal. *Why?*

## Back to Barfing

Josh and I were engaged for over a year before we set a wedding date. During this time, my eating disorder spun further out of control. I tried to get help from Josh and my family, but their attempts did nothing. In particular, my father's pitiful attempt was to tell me that, if anyone should have an eating disorder it should be him because he was the one always stressed out worrying about us five kids. I felt like screaming at him, "Oh, I'm so sorry for my existence." As usual, my father made it worse. I went to support groups with Josh, but the incessant blah, blah, blah didn't help either. Josh didn't know how to support me because I didn't know how to help myself. Quitting my eating disorder was ten times harder than quitting drinking, drugs, or smoking, and those things were hard. The basic human need to eat daily became one of the hardest things for me to do in a healthy manner. I could not understand how I had got to this point in my life.

I wasn't just skinny now, I was frail, but I still felt fat. If I could find an ounce of fat anywhere, I felt disgusting. I was in the worst mental state of my life. Many times, I thought about committing suicide, but never voiced those thoughts to anyone. While my insides screamed for help, everyone told me to eat food, don't throw up, do this and don't do that. They could not understand that it was not that easy. Their collective voices only made it worse. My eating disorder was slowly killing me. Never mind suicide; I was killing myself.

Right or wrong, good or bad, I would be the skinniest bride ever. The wedding preparations were awful for me. I didn't care about anything. I didn't want to be involved with anything. I wanted people to tell me when to show up, and I did. I wondered why I was so uninterested in my wedding. My insides told me that I wasn't doing the right thing and I felt trapped. I transferred my torment to my eating disorder. At least my barfing released something.

As the wedding date approached, I continued my slide. Two months before my wedding, I planned a dinner with my mom so we could have a heart to heart discussion about my situation. As we sat at the table she seemed concerned and asked me what was going on. *She didn't know?*

I blurted it out. "Mom, I'm going to be honest with you. I'm telling you this because if I go through with what I'm about to tell you, I would need you by my side and all your support. Mom, I want to call off the wedding. I can't get married to Josh. I need to get help and recover from my eating disorder before I think about getting married. Mom, besides wanting to recover from my eating disorder, I don't think Josh is my soul-mate. I think I'm making a mistake. Mom, I need you to help me call off my wedding. Mom, will you support me?"

My mother should be the one person to understand this, but my mom knew nothing about soul-mates since she was married to a man who abused her emotionally and physically. However, I didn't have anyone else to go to. I reasoned that, whether she agreed with me or not, my mother would want to see her child happy. Boy, was I wrong.

My mom launched the speech I least wanted to hear. "Alyson, you can't call off your wedding. You're nervous and getting cold feet. It's normal. Josh is a great guy and you'll have a wonderful happy life. Trust me."

Tormented, tired, and now confused, I continued to pour my heart out. "Mom, I don't want to settle for Josh. He's not my soul-mate. I know he's a great guy, but I think he's someone else's great guy. I'm stuck with a mental disease that's consuming me. This isn't the right time to go through such a life-changing event. I want to be fully present and mentally healthy when I get married."

My mother continued, "Alyson, we already have friends and family coming for the wedding. I would hate for them to waste money on plane tickets they've already bought. Josh is a great guy and he loves you dearly. I think it would be the wrong decision to call off the wedding."

My heart sank. There it was. Family and friends were more important than me. My impending death from an eating disorder didn't seem to matter. I left dinner devastated, went to my secret corner, and sought refuge in my eating disorder. Barfing was the one comfort I had left. The only choice I felt I had was to live my life with the eating disorder and to use Josh as my cover.


## The Wedding

I went to my wedding as the skinniest bride ever, and was happy about that. I rose before dawn and did a 50-kilometer run with some friends. That was my pre-ceremony celebration. Josh, on the other hand, had been out drinking with his friends the night before. I showed up flush with fresh air and Josh showed up still flushing. Yes, we had grown apart.

The last time I had a drink was the night of my Fourteener finish party, and I was sticking to my vow to never drink again. Despite massive peer pressure, I was a few years sober. A fast 50k run before my wedding was mandatory. I celebrated through running and being active, not drinking.

As I was dressing for my sacred vows, my father came into my room with a bottle of Dom Perignon. As I suspected, my father was not strong enough to quit drinking. He had broken his vow and wanted me to drink with him.

I wanted nothing to do with booze, and said, "What? You know I vowed to never take another drink three years ago. Just because you want to drink doesn't mean I have to. You want me to drink when I've struggled so hard to stay sober? Does this mean anything to you?"

As usual, my father had it backwards. I sat there partially dressed and stared at him in amazement. Again, it hit me that the only way he could cope was to make me be like him. That, I could never do. Then, with a twinkle, it hit me that I should stop calling him father and revert to calling him dad like I did when I was a child. That way, no matter which way it was spelled, it would be backwards. This thought was too sophisticated for my dad, so I tucked it into a private corner of my brain.

After I quit drinking, I caught hell from family and friends who wanted me to drink with them. Even Josh didn't like that I wouldn't drink with him. Recovered alcoholics understand that I can't have a couple drinks, and I was the only recovered alcoholic around. My dad made me feel I was defective for not drinking.

The wedding was beautiful. During the ceremony, my body was there, but my soul was running free through mountains. I tried to laugh it off, but it wasn't funny. Then, almost everyone forgot about me and got drunk. I was one of the few people who refused to drink at the reception. There I was, sober and married.

I understood why people go through with weddings even when they don't want to. I was scared as hell to break Josh's heart, upset my family, and devastate my friends. My family loved Josh. If I left him, it would take a long time for them to forgive me. I rationalized that I would go through life with Josh, and it would be fine. I kept telling myself I would be fine.

Toward the end of the reception, I was exhausted. I had gotten up early to do my run, and it had been a nonstop day. People were starting to leave and they were discussing which bar to go to afterwards. Josh asked me to go to the bar to drink and hang out with his friends and family. It was our wedding night. It was late. I had been around drunken people all day. Josh was drunk. I declined his invitation, left the wedding, and went home alone. Josh's parents gave me a ride and dropped off stuff from the reception. After they left, I looked around the quiet house. Presents filled our kitchen. Then I spotted the remains of our huge wedding cake. I thought, "Oh no! Not on my wedding night."

It was the cake and me. I was drained and didn't know if I even had the energy left to barf, but I was depressed. *Why was my husband not with me? Why did he not take me home, carry me inside, and make passionate love to me?* I felt alone and empty. That night, I felt more alone and dejected than I ever had. I felt more than ever that I had made my worst decision by marrying Josh.

Flooded with my dismal thoughts, I went for the cake. I ate the entire thing, then threw up. I was ashamed, sad, and confused. The blessing was that no one saw me do it, but that was part of the problem. Rolling on the floor in my fancy clothes, I didn't know what to do. I had gotten married and was already wondering how I could get out of it. I didn't know how to live authentically, and I didn't know how to overcome my eating disorder. I felt I had settled and, in despair, I felt the prospect of ignoring my true self was something I could never do.


## Married Life

Josh and I went to Alaska for our honeymoon. I agreed to go on a fishing trip with him if I could run the Anchorage Marathon. He agreed, and I was happy with the compromise. Our honeymoon was a week after our wedding. We had eight days planned in Alaska with many outdoor activities on the agenda. When we arrived, my eating disorder still haunted me. For a variety of obvious reasons, I didn't want anything to do with it on the trip, but the thoughts consumed me and comforted my emotions.

Every day, I got up early and went running. Josh slept in and did his own morning thing. I got back to our rented condo around noon, then we did something together. I battled increasing feelings that our relationship wasn't right. I wasn't right, so how could any relationship be right?

I enjoyed Alaska's beauty, but even views of that wild land could not cure my eating disorder. I was happy when the honeymoon ended. I had been alone more than half the time and that didn't feel like a honeymoon. I loved Alaska and pined over thoughts of going back one day with my fantasy soul-mate to run around in the mountains.

With our honeymoon over, we began the promised married life. I felt no different, just trapped and condemned to the life I was now living. Of course, questions from family and friends arose about when Josh and I were going to have children. I didn't want kids, and didn't want to be a mother. I made it clear that was how I felt, but still caught massive grief. I was a bad person for not wanting to be a mother and for not wanting to join all the drinking. It all made no sense. My family and friends didn't have enough life experience to understand that motherhood is not for everyone. Despite countless examples to the contrary, some assumed that everyone should have children even if they don't want them. Considering my own example, the children end up paying in the long run. As far as my dad was concerned, it was my duty to have children.

During our first year of marriage, I felt sad, upset, and lonely. On the weekends, Josh and I continued to do our own thing. Josh went biking with his friends, and I would go to the mountains with my hiking friends or run marathons with my running friends. Josh and I were like roommates and good friends, not two people in love, and not husband and wife.

The swirling snow and my thoughts tortured me. Prakash was still gone. All I had were serious questions. *If I live through this ordeal, am I going to listen to my heart and live for Alyson? Will I stand for what I believe and not settle for anything but true love and a soul-mate?*

I brushed crusted snow from my parka hood and listened for answers. Nothing but wind. My vision was partially blocked by my hood, and I couldn't turn my neck far to look for JB. I tried to cry out for my dog but, again, the wind stole my breath.

It was time for a higher power. I shut my eyes and talked to God. He was the only one there. Some might call it prayer, but I needed to make promises to someone so I blurted out my feelings.

I told God, "First take care of JB. Even if I die, let JB live. If I live through this ordeal, I'm going to change my life. I'm going to get divorced, then I'm going to control my eating disorder. The divorce will be tough, but it will also give Josh a chance for a better life with someone more normal. I need someone who is abnormal. I need someone who shares my obsessive, compulsive, and just-plain-nuts tendencies. I want to be with a mountain climber, an ultra-runner, and a nature lover; someone who always wants to be outdoors enjoying nature's beauty. I want someone who can see the value of living out your passions. I want someone to love me for what and who I am. I don't want someone who tries to change or shape me into their idea of the appropriate Alyson. I want to help other people who feel trapped in the same cycle of abuse and self-abuse. If I could save one person, this agony would be worthwhile."

I thought of my dear friends, Jim and Cappy, and how much their support and kindness meant to me. I wanted to be able to do the same for someone else. I released my pact with God to the wind, and looked for Prakash. Again, nothing. I tried to move, but only found stabbing pain. I drifted back to my thoughts.

# Chapter 12 – My Best Friend

All the road marathons I was running were on pavement, and the consistent impact was doing a number on my body. With injuries and constant soreness setting in, I realized that I couldn't do road running for the rest of my life, so I searched for races on trails. I found a 50k trail race close to my home and decided to give it a shot to see if ultra-distance running on dirt would be better for my body. With my love of mountains, I wondered if it would be more fun as well. Like my first marathon, that 50k race changed my life.

It was spectacular, and I was hooked. All dirt, little soreness, and running five miles farther than I had ever raced all seemed like something from a dream.

The race consisted of four eight-mile loops. This is where I met Chris. I make friends with strangers, and when Chris and I started talking, we couldn't stop. I didn't have many girlfriends, since I couldn't find any other women who wanted to do the activities I lusted for. The more I talked to Chris, the more I realized he had a passion for running, hiking, and serious mountain climbing. He felt like a partner, and a kindred mountain soul-mate. Chris and I found each other after the race and exchanged contact information. Meeting Chris was great, and I thought I could now have a friend for both the activities I enjoyed most.

*Had I finally met my match? A friend who would run marathons and ultra-distance races with me? A friend who liked getting up early to climb as many peaks as possible?* I cried, "Yes, I think he is the one."

After the race, Chris and I became close friends and indeed went hiking, running, and peak bagging together. I adored him because he was someone who had one of the kindest hearts I had ever known. Chris told me that he did not believe in God and lived by being a good person. At first, this bothered me because I thought, *What kind of person doesn't believe in God?* After getting to know Chris better, his beliefs didn't matter because he was an incredible person.

I introduced Chris to my husband, and Josh liked him. Almost all my friends were males, so Josh never had a problem with me having guy friends. Sometimes, this bothered me. Was I dispensable?

Alyson and Chris

After that first 50k race, I wanted more ultra-running action. My next progression into the ultra-distances would be a 50-miler. The increase from the marathon's 26.2 miles to the 50k's 31 miles was less than a five-mile increase, but the difference between a 50k and a 50 miler required a whopping 19-mile increase. After I did this calculation, I first thought that running 50 miles sounded nuts. However, I was nuts, and someone out there would tell me that I couldn't do it, so therefore I had to do it.

Chris and I planned on doing a self-supported, 50-mile run starting from the top of Monarch Pass. This seemed both absurd and exactly what I should do. During our preparations, Chris told me about organized 50-mile events and some 100-mile races. At first, I thought that there was no way someone could run 100 miles. Then, Chris told me about his dream to run the Leadville 100-mile race. He told me that Leadville was one of the first 100-mile races and still one of the hardest. Its high-altitude course crossed severe mountainous terrain. After hearing this, I thought Chris was nuttier than me. However, since crazy was our watchword, I realized that his dream was not a joke. I tucked the 100-mile thought deep inside my head and knew I had to complete the 50-mile objective first.

For our first 50-mile run, Chris and I invited Josh along for companionship and support. He would camp at the trailhead with us, then ride his mountain bike on our course to see how we were holding up. The night before our run, Chris wanted to sleep outside under the stars. I also loved sleeping outside, so I decided to join Chris. I asked Josh if he would join us outside, but he declined and opted to sleep in the car. Sleeping under the stars with another man while my husband was in the nearby car didn't feel right to me. What wasn't right was that Josh, my husband, didn't want to be near me.

Chris and I had an amazing 50-mile run together, and it changed me. Chris lifted me to a higher place. I had never run a distance like this before, and it showed me that I could do anything. Now, on the surface, the Leadville 100 still seemed crazy but, deep down, it felt possible. Perching on my higher place, I told Chris that I would one day run the Leadville 100 with him.

On our run, Chris and I talked about everything. I opened my heart and told him about my past and my dreams for the future. I told Chris about my goal of writing a book and becoming a motivational speaker. He told me that if there was anyone out there who could do it, it was me. Chris told me that I was one of a kind and was here to inspire and change people's lives. I believed him.

Chris gave me the courage to say that I could achieve my dream, and to go for it, since we get one chance at life. Chris was my mountain climbing partner, my ultra-running partner, and my best friend. He was wise beyond his years and as kind as they come. Being around him made me feel inspired and hopeful. Chris made me see life. Before Chris, I had been living with blinders on. Chris saw through my facade and called me forward many times. We shared a deep friendship and partnership, one that I had not even dreamed about.

In our time together, I shared my soul with Chris. I revealed my fears, passions, feelings, thoughts, desires, deepest—and sometimes darkest—secrets. My partner became everything and, on many climbs, I trusted Chris with my life.

Chris shared his prior life with me. He had been married for the past decade and recently divorced. He said that, over time, he grew apart from his wife. Chris loved the outdoors and climbing, but his wife became the exact opposite. I understood where he was coming from and this made our bond even stronger. Then, he told me about his girlfriend, an amazing woman whom he described as his soul-mate. He met Carolyn Wallace in Ouray on an ice-climbing trip. She lived and worked out of the country, so he did not see her much. I met Carolyn on one of her visits, and she was indeed an incredible woman.

I felt blessed and fortunate to see that kind of relationship and love. I knew it was out there. I knew that a soul-mate was possible. I had never met anyone who had a heart like Chris and assumed we would be friends forever. Then he was gone, and my world flipped upside down.

I had never lost a close friend like Chris, and had no idea how to deal with the emotions of loss. Nothing was the same. I didn't want to run or hike. I wanted to cry. I shut down. This lasted for a month before I crawled out of my emotions and continued living like I knew Chris wanted me to. I ran and climbed as a way to talk to Chris. He was now my guardian angel.

# Chapter 13 – Dying

I didn't know if I was shivering or shaking from my deep thoughts about Chris. It was only three months since he had died, and my memories haunted me on this wretched slab. *What had happened to my guardian angel?* Chris wasn't here to help me. I had been living like Chris wanted me to, active and trying to overcome my eating disorder, but here I lay, broken, bleeding, and freezing. *Was I to die and join him?*

As my shaking subsided into shivering, I tried to get control of my breathing. A few minutes dribbled by, and my shivering slowed. When it stopped, I let my breathing slow as well. This was different; something was wrong. I tried to rev up my breathing to get enough energy to twitch. I couldn't do it and, to my amusement, it didn't matter anymore.

Calm, I felt Chris with me. I knew he wouldn't let me give up without giving it everything I had. I owed it to Chris. I owed it to myself. *I have to make it through this. I have to live. But, how?*

My reality was orbiting somewhere around me now. I had lost too much blood. I had lost too much heat. Too much time had passed. Prakash was gone and there was no rescue. When my positive thoughts floated free with my resolve, I kissed them goodbye. Even my pain was fading. When none of it mattered, I found an inner peace inside my broken body.

In a trance, quiet tranquility flowed. Then, a bright light blazed behind my closed eyes. I welcomed the light, knowing it was God coming to take me. Thoughts, memories, and reality were no longer important. I wasn't afraid. What was left of me swirled toward the brightening light. As I transcended, the slab and mountain came with me in a final homage. We were no longer part of the Earth. I looked down on Mount Rosalie, and we saluted each other. I still loved the mountain.

I was going to Heaven. I would see Chris soon. When I reached Heaven, I could no longer disappoint my father or be married to Josh, and I could no longer not be authentic. There is no faking it in Heaven. I was ready to bare my soul before my maker and beg for mercy. With my spirit about to leave my body, something unearthly happened. God spoke directly to me.

God told me that I would not die now. He told me that I had to stay on Earth, be authentic, and that he would give me the strength to survive. God gave me a second chance.

From that moment, with every ounce of life left in me, I knew I had to survive. The rescue would be painful and difficult, but I knew that somewhere inside me I still had the strength and will to survive. My ascent to Heaven stopped abruptly, and I fell back onto my slab.

# Chapter 14 – In For A Bumpy Ride

Far away, I heard the sound of breathing. *What the hell is that?* Louder now, I heard a swish of snow that a boot in motion makes, then I heard an unmistakable voice. Prakash was back.

Prakash checked on me then scurried over to a nearby rock rim to look down into the valley. Once on the rim, he screamed, "I see lights."

I breathed, "Oh my God, lights."

Prakash hollered again, "They're only 500 feet below us." He hurried back to me and added, "But it might take them a couple hours to get to us."

I felt a new sense of hope and prayed that JB could hold on for that long. At least he could curl into a tight warmth-saving ball.

Prakash dashed back to the rim and called SAR to inform them he saw them and let them know what to look for. He started a strobe on one headlamp and placed it on a rock to guide the rescue team. He also turned on an avalanche beacon to transmit our location since visibility was so poor, turned on another red headlamp, and began blowing a whistle. He spent the next hour getting up to sing and whistle for the rescuers, jumping up and down to generate body heat before coming back to check on me.

I was back to shivering. I had taken my mittens off, pulled my arms into my parka, and was trying to get my hands into my armpits. This complicated maneuver didn't work well, and I was tangled up. Prakash fished his hands out of his gloves, untangled my clothing mess, and helped me put my mittens back on. Pure adrenaline kept Prakash's hands from freezing, since he had a set of torn ski gloves and no hand warmers. I couldn't understand how adrenaline could work for so long. *Divine intervention?* Then, Prakash cuddled next to me to block the wind, and said, "How's my new best friend doing?"

After another trip to the rock rim, he seemed puzzled, and reported that the lights we saw earlier were gone. *Gone?* Shouting was useless in the wind. Prakash came back to me and, remaining positive, we reasoned that they must be hidden by a nearby hump.

Prakash took up his usual spot next to me, and we huddled a little longer.

After what seemed like another hour, it was time for another SAR call. This time, Prakash had to dial with the tip of his nose since his fingers had lost sensation.

"Hey, this is Prakash calling about the Alyson rescue situation. Do you have an update?"

"What? We started a new shift. I'm the new person"

"Oh, okay. Sorry. We're up here on Mount Rosalie trying to get rescued, and we're looking for an update on where the teams are."

"You should only call us when you need to. The teams are coming."

We were both confused about where the rescue team could have gone, and I tried hard to remain calm. I had no energy for much else anyway. Time had long since run out for both of us.

Back in motion scouting, Prakash finally saw three lights. He ran to the strobe, picked it up, and swung it above his head singing, "This little light of mine, I'm gonna let it shine, let it shine, let it shine, let it shine." Even though I was near death, the song, his voice, and enthusiasm cheered me. Prakash also blew loud blasts on his whistle in hopes that the singing, whistle, or strobe light would get their attention.

Then, out of the white abyss, JB thought he needed to join the party. My dog came to me, and it was the first time I had been able to touch him for many hours. Our joyful reunion elevated both of us to a new level. With all the commotion, JB knew something was going on and, with his keen dog instincts, he knew it was something good. JB went over to the dancing and singing Prakash, saw the lights approaching, and began his fierce black lab bark. That did it. That bark would attract attention anywhere. My rescuers were having a party.

Suddenly, I could see the lights and knew they were minutes away. Now, everything I had been preparing for all night was about to happen. Huge questions still hung in the wind. *Would I be able to get down this mountain alive? How bad would my pain get? Did they bring pain medication?*

Prakash continued his ritual of heading out and signaling every few minutes. If they went off track after being so close, we would have died furious. Prakash kept returning to me to make small talk, get my spirits up, and prepare me for what lay ahead.

Moments later, they arrived. Prakash was so excited to greet members of the Alpine Rescue Team, that he shouted, "Woohoo! What's up, guys? Breezy up here, yes?"

He got a simple reply, "You bet it is."

Prakash continued, "Did you hear me singing very badly?"

"Yes, we did."

The wind howled at a sustained 50 miles per hour, carrying a load of horizontal snowflakes. A woman rescuer came to me, introduced herself as Lynda, and chatted in a cheerful tone, but she had to shout over the wind. For me, her voice sounded like an angel. Lynda was the certified medic on the team. When she tried to examine me, conditions were so bad that all three rescuers knew they had to get me down fast. Lynda continued talking while the others prepared me for movement.

Lynda had done her homework and asked me what kind of sports I was interested in. Coming back to life, I told her that ultra-running and mountain climbing were my two favorite sports. Lynda was an ultra-marathoner too, and we had an instant ultra-athlete connection. When the guys started to move me a little bit, my pain made a dramatic reappearance. She kept me distracted, and we made running plans on the spot, which helped to take my mind off the pain.

Lynda continued, "Yeah, I did the Leadville 100 last year. It was fun."

I perked up, "What? I love you. What was your time?"

"Twenty-eight hours. I'm trying to get under 25 next year so they'll give me a nice big belt buckle I can wear with my tiny black dress."

"I want to sign up for that next year." I know Lynda probably thought I would be lucky if I could walk again, but she nodded and smiled. I wanted to run a marathon with her. I thought how selfless she was. *Did she know how much her words helped me?*

Prakash interrupted, "Aly, I thought you were going to try knitting for the next couple years."

Lynda laughed. "Actually, she should take up crocheting. A friend of mine found knitting to be a little dangerous with those sharp needles."

The second rescuer fished out a tarp that they put over me to block the wind and snow while they prepared a litter to haul me in. Their litter was a blow-up stretcher made for backcountry situations where a rigid litter was too heavy and impractical.

In the commotion, I shouted, "Somebody needs to take care of Prakash. He gave me all his clothes."

Prakash insisted, "Alyson... don't worry about me... relax and breathe... I'm fine."

Now, the next thing on my mind was to get pain medication before they moved me. "Someone brought morphine, right?"

Lynda told me that they had no drugs, that only certified paramedics could give drugs like morphine, and that I had to get down without drugs. I felt sick. I couldn't believe what they were telling me. "Nothing? Really? Nothing?"

Lynda bent close and said, "Alyson, this is likely to be the most painful thing you're ever going to endure. You're strong, you're a survivor. I just met you, and I know you can do this."

I looked into her gentle face and met her eyes. I thought how kind she was. I thought what she was doing was amazing. I wanted to be able to help save people too. I wanted to believe her words were really for me and not rehearsed language for a person on the verge of dying. Her eyes told me she meant what she had said. I was a survivor.

All at once, it hit me. *I was going to make it.* I am strong. I had spent my life climbing my personal mountain of despair. I reached the peak and fell hard. The accident had tried my soul but from that peak, I had looked back down on my old life below. I thought of everything I had survived before the fall, and realized I was strong all along. I just hadn't known it.

The rescuers gathered and talked about how they were going to lift me onto the litter. They said that the faster I got on the litter, the less pain I would suffer. Lynda had determined that, based on the location of my pain, my femur was broken.

When they were ready to make the transfer, the leader shouted, "Three, two, one, lift!"

What strength I had left completely exploded. With power from beyond, I screamed and then breathed. The next command came, "Lower."

I screamed again and then out of breath, I moaned.

The lifting actually felt like being in a nightmare; it was sheer torment. When they lowered me, I felt like I was being tortured; it was pure agony. My pain was limitless. Everyone there watched, listened, and suffered as well. Then, I heard them talking. There had been a slight miscommunication during the lift-transfer-lower routine, the sleeping bag on the litter was not below me, and I had to be lifted again.

My shrieking pleas were wretched for the rescuers and devastating for Prakash. In preparation for the new transfer, a rescuer asked Prakash if he could say something to console me. Prakash came to me, bent close, and spoke in my ear so that I would recognize his voice.

"Alyson, remember what I told you about the pain?"

"Ah. Something about inflammation?"

"Are you breathing? Are you relaxed?" Prakash tried to remind me about the yogic breathing technique.

"Yes."

I breathed as Prakash instructed, and it helped calm me. My frozen-fingered, one-eyed Prakash stood over me and smiled in admiration. The second litter transfer was tough but, with more helping hands, it was not as bad as the first one.

A rescuer patted Prakash on the shoulder, "Good job up here."

Prakash mumbled, "Nah, thanks for coming out tonight. She's my friend, but we're strangers to you. You came out into hell for us."

"It's our pleasure," he responded. "We live for this. By the way, you've a huge dollop of ice hanging from your eyebrow. I don't want to pull it because your eyebrow might come off with it."

"Nah, I kind of like it there," Prakash replied.

Once I was secure in the litter-bag that formed around my body, my pass-out pain decreased but, still high on the mountain, I could not fathom how I would deal with this pain all the way down. This was Hell, and Heaven now seemed like a better option. I don't know if anyone heard me, but I muttered, "God, please. Take me now. I can't handle this much pain."

Then, I remembered that God said he would give me enough strength to survive. While the rescuers prepared to move, I calmed my brain and reversed my thought process. Still talking to myself, I said, "Remember to breathe. Inhale. Remember what Prakash told you: think hospital bed." *I am strong. I can do this.*

Prakash and the rescuers lifted me, and the slowest decent of my life began. It was a communal journey now, with my rescuers working hard and Prakash post-holing off to the side with JB, while I endured, screaming. More rescuers surged uphill toward us through the trees. The full power of the amazing Alpine Rescue Team was now in motion with me. From the chatter, I learned there were more than six organizations involved in my rescue. Bouncing along down the mountain, I started to drift in and out of consciousness.

Two feet of fresh snow covered the rocks, and the wind sent the snow into all the pits between the rocks. The footing for the rescuers was slippery, but they did a phenomenal job of controlling the litter in the snow, wind, and dark. A four-person litter carry is difficult on a paved parking lot but, here, it resembled a teetering creep. Then two more rescuers arrived, and we had a six-person carry. This was much better since it's a given that, in these conditions, two will always be stumbling, but that leaves four to control the litter.

There was inevitable jostling, and my pain sent me to another world. My screams were involuntary. I was no longer sure that the screams were even coming from me.

I knew my cries had to be heart-wrenching for the rescuers, Prakash, and JB, who was so concerned for his mommy that he dashed around the litter, zipping between the rescuers' legs. I knew JB was making the rescue harder, but I was so busy screaming that my calls to him were pitiful. He could tell that his mommy was in big trouble, and he would not relax until I was safe. I was comforted that JB was moving well and would survive. The rescuers commented that it was amazing to watch the loyal connection between JB and me. I think my dog's energy helped everyone, even though his between-the-legs dashing made the footing trickier for the rescuers.

We had a mile of descent over snow-covered rocks to reach treeline where the terrain became easier and a rigid litter was waiting. This would become the monster mile I could never forget. An inch is as good as a mile? No, not here. Every inch sent my orbiting pain into unexplored domains, and there were tens of thousands of inches to endure. In my state, that was infinity.

The rescuers were moving me down the mountain headfirst. The logic for this position was to both elevate my broken leg and put it out of harm's way. I understood the logic, but this left my head in harm's way. The rescuers had covered me with a tarp to protect me from the cold and falling snow. This was fine except that, in the confusion and dark, my head would slip unseen out from under the tarp, escape the litter-bag, and bang along on the snow-covered rocks. I couldn't see enough to make any sense of what might come next, and any movement to improve my position rearranged my pains. Every icy boulder bump transferred straight to my still-shifting, broken bone.

My mind started screaming as well. "Please God, make it stop. Please! Stop! I want morphine. Anything!"

Ironically, when I really needed a drug, there were none available. My cries became vocal. "I want my mom. Stop! Mom! Morphine! Mom! Stop!" My mother was the only person I wanted right now. My cries were fueled by a natural instinct and my history. Of course, my mom was not there to help. My multiple mommies right now were the rescuers moving me down the mountain. They carried and pulled me despite my cries of pain. My life was in their hands, and if they obeyed my command to stop, I would die.

Gratitude would come later, but in my dazed state I listened to their constant exchanges and realized they were working hard and still being efficient. In this horrible struggle, efficiency was speed. They were the ones out after midnight above treeline in a raging blizzard moving a screaming stranger down over snow-covered rocks. They were the ones working hard and risking their own safety. They were the ones who were saving my life. All I had to do was endure. Consumed by pain, I could not express my growing sense of gratitude for these faceless strangers. Maybe it was God's promise or the new strength within me, but I knew I had to survive so I could thank them.

The rocks were bigger lower down, and the last 500 feet to the trees took so long that I was sure that hell was freezing over. In spite of the jostling and screaming, I was getting colder. In spite of my rescuer's efforts, I could still die. Finally, on one sideways lurch, I saw a tree.

There were new voices now, and I couldn't keep track of everything going on. I knew I would get transferred to a hard litter, and that would create new pain. I thought that, just as I knew what pain to expect, it would vault to a new level.

Poor Prakash. His prescription glasses were iced over and useless. He shoved them into his shell, but then rime coated his eyelashes and eyebrows. His right eye froze open, and he could only see out of his left eye. Prakash knew that his problems were minor compared to mine.

The descent through the trees brought new challenges. The rocks were gone, but the snow was deeper. Part of the team snowshoed down, breaking a wide trail for the litter team. It was exhausting work, but more rescuers came through the forest to relieve the current team. Once relieved, a team would take a short break, then catch up and take over again. Through it all, radios crackled.

Even partially aware, my sense of gratitude for these volunteer rescuers grew. I had interrupted their Saturday night, and they continued to operate like a well-oiled machine. They were amazing, selfless people. I felt an energy shift in my body, and my self-pity vanished. They saved me and their only reward was the satisfaction of getting me off the mountain. How could I ever thank them enough? I was determined to take control of my life and do something to help make this a better place. I had to take my second chance at life and do something to change the world even just for one person. I owed them that much.

Even with a tarp covering my face, I smelled and heard a roaring fire. Disoriented and confused, I asked a rescuer where we were. He told me we were a mile above the trailhead where they had built a fire for relief. We paused for a few minutes, they opened my tarp, and I felt the first external heat since my last hand warmer had expired many hours earlier. I asked the rescuer where Prakash and JB were. He told me they had moved ahead and were down at the trailhead getting warmed up. I was relieved.

Another rescuer told me that my husband Josh was also at the trailhead. Even in my pain and continuing agony, the thought of seeing Josh sent my mind spinning. A few hours earlier, I had promised God that I would divorce Josh. A touch of the reality that waited for me crept in. How was I going to end my marriage? It would be difficult. Would my family forgive me? Only time would tell, and wasting energy on the details would not help me get off this mountain. I still needed morphine.

I belted out, "For the love of God, can someone tell me how long it's going to be until I can get some pain medicine?"

I got a sympathetic reply. "Alyson, we have a half mile until we reach the snowmobile team. That team has paramedics, and they have drugs for you. Hang in there."

With a degree of sarcasm, I answered, "Well, I have no intention of running off now do I?" I shouldn't have said it, but I was beyond being polite. I had been tortured for hours and could not bear to think of the agonizing pain continuing. I wished I could take the words back. I hoped they understood.

Finally, I could hear the snowmobiles. There were new people here including the paramedics with morphine. All we had to do was get it into me. The paramedics wanted to inject the morphine through a vein in my arm. I was wearing five jackets at the time, and the only way I could get the drug was if I they cut the jackets to expose my arm. A paramedic asked if he could cut the jackets and, for a tenth of a second, I tried to compute the clothing's value. In the next tenth, I said, "Yes. Hurry."

The morphine ripped through my body, and my calculation ended after a few seconds. The relief was as dramatic as any experience I had ever had, and I knew the rest of my nightmare would be easy. The paramedics in the ambulance at the trailhead would have IV drugs that would finally end the pain.

The bumps on the snowmobile ride still sent shocking pain through my morphine haze, but I knew that a hospital bed waited for me. Prakash would be at the trailhead, along with my black lab. I hoped they were okay. With a whoosh, we arrived at the trailhead.

I cried out, "I did it. I made it. I survived it all." Then, I heard a familiar voice.

"Sweetie, I'm right here. You're going to be fine. I love you."

I burst into tears when I heard Josh. He, Prakash, and JB watched the paramedics load me into the ambulance. I couldn't talk, but knew they were fine and they knew I was in good hands.

In the ambulance, the paramedics asked numerous questions about my injuries. They needed to figure out what was broken and call the hospital to tell them what to expect. A paramedic grabbed scissors and started cutting off my pants. I had two pairs of long underwear under my snow pants. The paramedic wiggled all three layers off without causing me too much distress, but I did let loose a few yelps.

Looking at my left leg, it was clear what I had been dealing with. The sight made me quiver. My broken femur had bent my thigh into a grotesque shape. The paramedics were concerned about the amount of blood I had lost internally. They said that the freezing temperatures may have saved my life. I thought yes, but Prakash really saved my life. Without giving it a second thought, he put his own life at risk to save mine. Since Prakash gave me extra clothes, I had no hypothermia or frostbite, just some frostnip. As the ambulance rolled toward the hospital, I thought that this accident was both the worst and the best thing that could have happened to me. Balance, moderation, freedom, flexibility, change, and other possibilities danced in my mind. Thanks to Prakash and my rescuers, I had a future to consider.

# Chapter 15 – Coming Back To Life

I awoke freezing, shivering, and scared. I had no idea where I was, but the room I was in was brighter than any room I had ever seen. For a fleeting flash, I thought I had completed my white light transcendence and was in Heaven. In the next flick, reality rushed in, and I wondered what had happened to me. *How could I be so cold?* I remembered that I was tired of being cold.

On reflex, I freaked out and shouted, "Where am I?" A nurse entered the room, saw me shivering, grabbed a blanket, and wrapped it around me. I was in a hospital bed, but had no memory of this place. After a few minutes, I calmed down enough to ask, "What happened? Why am I here?"

The nurse explained my accident and said I had undergone surgery. The anesthesia explained why I was confused about where I was and what had happened to me. The nurse said she would move me and get me settled into my room where I would stay until I could leave the hospital.

Time came near to a stop, and it felt like I was in that bright white room forever. As I refocused, I wanted to see my mom. The room was so antiseptic that I needed to hear a familiar voice to comfort me and tell me that everything was going to be okay.

Finally, another nurse came into the room, and asked, "Are you Alyson?"

I nodded my head yes.

"Hi, I'm Heidi, and I'll be taking care of you from here on out." Heidi had a soothing voice, and that centered me. Another nurse appeared and helped Heidi transport me to my new room. After they got me settled and arranged for the drugs to appear at regular intervals, I asked Heidi about my surgery. She said that I had a long titanium plate and rods put in my left leg. She said the surgery went well and now it was time to start thinking of recovery. *Recovery?* That thought seemed impossible at the moment. As she told me more about my accident, I started to regain the memory of my horrendous ordeal.

I had been immobile on the slab, and now I was immobile in my hospital bed. The thought of not being able to run or hike anymore weighed my spirit down like a Fourteener made of broken bricks. I tried to remain optimistic and thought about how great the extra time to write my book would be, but there was no fooling myself. I knew my recovery would be one of the hardest things I would ever have to do. My recovery was an extension of getting off the mountain alive. I was now on a new mountain.

My room was too quiet. *Where was my family? Where was my Mom? Where was Josh? Prakash? Did anybody care about me?* Tears began to find my eyes, I felt like an emotional basket case.

As I tried to gather my thoughts into something that made sense, I heard a knock on my door. Josh swooshed in with his hands full of flowers and a stuffed teddy bear. The beautiful flowers, with their mixture of colors and shapes, lightened my mood. The wonderful scent filled the room. The teddy bear held a heart that said, "I Love You," and that touched my heart. After Josh gave me the teddy bear, he knelt and kissed me. His soft warm lips against mine made me feel loved. Someone did care. The kiss made me question how I could ever hurt this person who had been so good to me. Josh truly loved me.

I remembered the promises that I made to God and myself a few hours earlier. My spinning emotions were hard to explain. I loved Josh. I still wondered why I didn't think of him while I was trapped on the mountain. Well, I did think of him, just not in the way that I would have hoped for. *Why didn't I want him beside me?* I did love Josh. *Why wasn't that enough to stay married to him?* I knew the answer, and I knew what I had to do. Josh deserved to find true love as much as I did. It would not be fair to him or me if we stayed in the marriage. I knew the only way I would ever be happy was to find my soul-mate. I knew he existed. I knew he was out there. I knew I had to try. Even stuck in my hospital bed and facing a long recovery, I had one shot at life and would go for the highest summit of hope. I had already reached the pinnacle of despair and needed to put that peak far behind me. Mount Rosalie became my shrine to the end of one tortured life and the beginning of a new one with hope.

Josh pulled up a chair and sat next to me, holding my hand. I was medicated at this point and emotional. What I had been through the day before was surreal. It seemed like a dream from which I would emerge at any moment. However, what happened was not a dream, and I had a leg full of stitches and a titanium plate to prove it. I asked Josh where my family was and if they were going to be here soon. He said that my mom, brothers, and sister would soon be here. I waited in anticipation.

Stuck in my bed, time seemed to drag. I asked Josh about JB, and he said our dog was shaken by the ordeal but that he was going to be fine. That thought brought tears to my eyes. *My boy, he was there for me and wouldn't leave me.* I loved him like a son. I asked how Prakash was doing, and Josh told me Prakash was well and waiting to see me. I told Josh about Prakash's efforts during the wait and the rescue.

I was given a second chance and felt an enormous amount of gratitude and grateful to be alive. I asked Josh if my dad planned to come and told him that I didn't think it was a good idea. My dad could bring the mood down in any situation. After what happened, I couldn't handle his negativity.

I said straight out, "Please Josh, if my dad plans to come, talk him out of it. If he insists, tell him that there is no negativity allowed in this room. Otherwise, he's not welcome. That's an order." Josh, who was close with my dad, understood. After I said this, I knew my dad would come. Telling him to not do something was a guarantee that he would do it.

My nurse, Heidi came in and said, "Alyson, my shift is almost over and a nighttime nurse will take care of you. I'll be back early tomorrow and will see you then. Several TV people came by today and wanted to interview you. I told them it was not possible today, but maybe later this week. I wanted to talk to you about this first. What do you think?"

"Why do TV people want to interview me?"

"Your amazing rescue was a big deal and involved many people. The Flight for Life failure has raised questions about their policies and procedures. They want to get your side of the story."

I thought that some interviews would be fine and agreed to them later on, but not now. I was still feeling weak and emotionally drained. I also wanted to take a shower and brush my hair before I faced TV cameras, and I did not see how that was going to happen anytime soon. Shower? I couldn't yet imagine how I was going to get out of bed and stand up.

My night shift nurse walked into the room and introduced herself as Kim. She asked if I wanted to go to the bathroom. That meant being lifted onto a wheelchair, wheeled to the bathroom, and lifted onto the toilet seat. That seemed like a lot to just pee. The nurse said she could also bring a bedpan, and I wouldn't have to move at all. Neither of these plans seemed appealing. The good news was that I didn't need to go yet, since I hadn't had anything to eat or drink in over a day. However, my tummy was now growling.

I remembered my eating disorder and all the admonishments I had received to eat. I remembered my vow to overcome my disorder. Did it take this ordeal to make me hungry? Perhaps, and I now looked forward to taking my first steps to gaining some weight.

Before I could ask Kim what I would be able to eat, there was a knock on my door. My mom walked in followed by Sarah, Daniel, and Meggie. Meggie was engaged to my little brother, and she was a caring person who always brightened a room. Scanning for my youngest brother, I asked, "Where's Kyle?"

My mom explained, "He's not comfortable in hospitals and decided not to come. He says he's sorry and wishes you well."

This made me sad because Kyle and I were close. Why would he not want to be here with me? I had almost died. I realized it was more than he could emotionally handle. Looking back at my white light, I felt that I died and miraculously come back to life.

Sarah brought me a cute unicorn pillow, which was sappy sweet, and my new pet lifted my spirits. My mom, Daniel, and Meggie showered me with flowers and get-well balloons. Everything lightened the atmosphere and breathed cheer into my dumpy spirits. Once everyone was comfortable, they asked me questions. Sarah was the first to ask if I would tell the entire story. I was still trying to get the anesthesia out of my body and get something to eat. However, I knew that I had better get used to this question.

I walked my family through the entire day. At first, it was hard to remember what had happened but as I told the story, it all came back to me. From leaving the house in the morning with JB, meeting Kevin Baker at the trailhead, and my fall, to having my life flash before my eyes, and feeling that bright light take over my body and lift me away.

Telling the story made me emotional, and tears fell from my eyes like a waterfall. What were the tears from? I did not know. Were they tears of happiness to be alive or tears of sadness for my future? I wasn't sure what they meant, only that I felt every word that I said.

After I finished the story, a nurse came in to give me more pain medication. After she left, we got another knock on the door.

Worried that it might be my dad, I said, "Who is it?"

My older brother Jason and his wife Jonni came in. As a child, I had a great relationship with Jason, and we were close. However, in recent years, I did not get along with Jason or Jonni at all. I wanted to share my adventures with them, but they always thought I was bragging or, worse, that climbing was stupid. As they approached my bed and took a seat, they both appeared to have a bad attitude written across their faces.

I was never able to keep my mouth shut, so I spoke up. "Why did you guys even come? I almost lost my life, and the last thing I want in my hospital room is negativity."

Neither Jason nor Jonni said a word. They both looked rather surprised. I was on heavy pain meds and in an emotional state after telling my story. This was not a good time to speak my mind to family or, perhaps, with the truth blaring at me, it was the best time. In any case, there it was. I was not going to hold anything back and the flood gates opened.

I went on to let them have it for the next ten minutes. I poured out everything that had been on my mind for the past several years about our poor relationship. I had no censor in my mouth, but it felt good to speak the truth. Blame it on the drugs or situation, but my ordeal and promises now allowed me to speak freely, and I was grateful for the opportunity.

I thought that my family didn't need to hear my rant, and I apologized for that. After I shut my mouth, an awkward silence swallowed the room.

A nurse broke the spell by announcing that visiting hours were ending and everyone could return tomorrow. Everyone except Josh, who was going to sleep by my side in a chair.

My first night in the hospital was awful. I was uncomfortable with post-surgery pain. I was also full of emotional and mental torments. It felt awkward to have Josh in the room with me, and the night passed slowly.

Jim and Cappy visited early the next morning and that warmed my heart. They were both caring and wonderful, and lifted my spirits. Jim told me that he would do whatever he could to help me rehab. I knew he meant it, so it gave me high hopes to have a friend help me climb Mount Rehab. Jim and Cappy had been to many of my marathon races, so they knew I was an athlete and they knew I would do everything to come back from this injury.

After I visited with Jim and Cappy, a new nurse appeared and explained that a physical therapist would soon start me on the road to recovery. For starters, she would help me to stand up, get on crutches, and make it to the bathroom. We were dealing with baby steps here, but I still wasn't feeling well, and it all seemed a bit premature.

At first, the physical therapist seemed upbeat and professional. She talked me through what we were going to try to accomplish, and I told her that I would try my hardest to do everything she asked. My first task was to get out of bed and stand up. With help, I sat on the edge of the bed, but even this minor movement was painful, and I was a bit woozy. Next, I needed to place my feet on the ground and shift my weight to my feet. This made me, the runner of marathons and climber of peaks, nervous. I placed my feet on the ground and tried to stand up, but immediately fell back to the bed. Lightheaded and sick, I couldn't stand. Now nauseous, I couldn't do it. *Good grief, I couldn't even stand. Something was wrong.*

The physical therapist adopted a stern do-it attitude that made me feel worse. I was upset enough that I couldn't stand, and now I had a helper who didn't know how to help. If I wanted that, I would call my dad and tell him to come help.

I told the therapist that I would try one more time, and try I did. This time, as I weighted my feet, I fainted and fell back onto my bed where I was out cold for a few moments.

Now, the therapist knew something was wrong. "Alyson, are you okay?"

It took me a few minutes to come to and when I did, I asked for my main nurse. When Heidi came into the room, I told her what had happened and that I thought something was wrong. Still in my speak-out mode, I told her I wanted a new physical therapist. Heidi was on it, immediately called my doctor, and he decided to run several tests.

In my hours on Rosalie, I had bled internally, and by the time I reached the hospital, I had lost a lot of blood. The tests showed that I had not yet recovered from the blood loss, which was why I was lightheaded and having trouble standing up. The doctor ordered a blood transfusion, which I agreed to. A blood transfusion sounded serious, but I had to start by finding my feet.

Finally, it was just my surgeon and me in the room. He was a compassionate man, and I expressed gratitude for what he did for me during my operation.

Thoughtful, he answered, "Alyson, the femur is the biggest bone in the body and probably the hardest one to break. How do you think it happened?"

I knew the truth but didn't want to blurt it out. *Couldn't I just say that I slipped, fell, and it broke?* That was part of the truth, but in my new truth-telling mode, I couldn't tell a partial truth. I owed the doctor and myself the full truth because the truth was the only thing that would set me free. There was no better time to practice the truth than now, plus my smart surgeon knew that something else was up, and he was fishing for the truth.

I launched into my secret. "Doc, I suffered from anorexia and bulimia for many years. I had a bone density scan not long ago, and the results were bad. My bones are in the beginning stage of osteopenia. I'm sure that's why my femur broke so easily."

My doctor didn't seem surprised and he agreed that my eating disorder was likely the cause of my broken bone. He talked about thin weak bones and their associated problems. My doctor went on to say that if I wanted to be an athlete for the rest of my life, I better

140

think twice about living with an eating disorder. As my surgeon rose to leave, he left me with a simple thought that changed my life. He looked at me and said, "Alyson, you have a choice."

Alone with the medical truth parked in my lap, I thought about this for a moment. *My eating disorder almost took my life. Was I going to let it kill me?* Of course not. I had a choice. Suddenly, I was the strongest person I knew, and overcoming the eating disorder became my top priority.

I spent the rest of my second day at the hospital getting the blood transfusion and being in a strange place mentally and emotionally. I kept reminding myself that I was alive. I was heavily sedated and not sure what my true emotions were. *Were the drugs talking or were my real feelings sharper than ever? Did I make all those promises to myself on the mountain?* Of course, I did, but thoughts are cheap. Would I keep all of those promises, or would reality overwhelm me? While I lay in my hospital bed having more blood injected into my system, my thoughts consumed me. The long, slow process gave me more time to think about my problems, but I was so sick of sitting and thinking at this point, that all I wanted to do was jump up and go for a long run.

By the third day, I felt much better. The blood transfusion was a success, and now I was ready to start physical therapy. My new physical therapist was an older woman who had been doing PT for over 20 years. Nevertheless, our sessions were demanding. I had to learn to walk on crutches, and that was only the beginning. I needed to relearn how to walk, run, hike, and climb. Never mind my fancy promises, moving at all would be one of the most daunting tasks ahead of me.

Intent on my new journey, I figured out the crutches and made it 200 feet down the hall. The elevator door opened behind me and my family and Josh appeared. They turned toward my room, so I called them. I was excited to show my progress, and they were happy to see the improvements I had made in one day. My long crutch walk, however, had tired me out, so we retreated to my room where Josh and Daniel helped me back into bed.

After visiting, I asked a question that I had avoided. "Where's dad? Is he planning to come? I don't want him to come if he's going to be negative. I cannot handle that kind of atmosphere right now."

My mom said that my dad was in Phoenix for the weekend to visit his parents and that he would return later that evening. A visit would be up to him.

I made it clear. "Dad is not allowed in this room if he's going to be negative. If he's going to say I told you so or ask me when I'm going to grow up and stop climbing mountains, I don't want him in here. If he says those things, it will end our already tattered relationship. Please, Mom, if he decides he's going to come see me, talk to him first and tell him to be on good, positive behavior. No visit would be better than a negative visit. Mom, tell him that he has a choice."

There was a mountain of baggage and profuse pain buried within my relationship with my father. I didn't understand him, and I didn't understand how any parent on the planet could act like he always did. My mom said she would talk to him.

Numerous flowers, stuffed animals, and gifts appeared in my hospital room and they made me feel loved. Looking around, it saddened me that many of these things were from Josh's family. They were such caring and amazing people. How would I be able to hurt their son so deeply? Would my pursuit of true love make me the bad person? I waffled.

*Would I suck it up and stay married to Josh or was I going to stick to my guns and do everything I had promised myself?* God gave me a second chance and He helped me survive. I had already received the greatest divine intervention possible. The rest was up to me. I needed to focus on getting out of the hospital before I invested too much energy on what would happen next.

By day four, different news stations came to interview me about the accident and ensuing rescue. The interviews brought up the controversy with the Flight for Life procedures. The interviewers asked me why the Flight for Life team didn't leave me anything.

I said that the chopper was only on the ground for a minute, and that the nurses were in street clothes and shorts. It was their choice to hop back in the chopper without leaving us anything. No sleeping bag, tarp, extra clothes, medicine, nothing. When pressed,

I said I didn't even know if those items were in the chopper and that was a question for Flight for Life. I was, however, grateful and praised them for trying.

Later that evening, Josh and I watched the news and there I was on TV. I didn't like how I looked in a hospital gown, and without a shower, I did brush my hair.

I continued to improve on day four. My pain receded, and I focused my emotions and engaged in positive self-talk. My friend, Shawn, who I called from the mountain after the accident, and Prakash planned to see me that evening. I was excited to see them, but was also nervous. Prakash and I had been through something deep together that other people would not understand. He saved my life. He risked his own life for mine. I felt forever and profoundly indebted to him and intensely grateful to have someone in my life with such a kind heart. I tried to turn the nervous feelings into positive thoughts. I should be good at that by now.

That evening, as I ate dinner in my hospital bed, I heard a knock on the door and a friendly voice. I knew who it was and said yes, come in. There were Shawn and Saint Prakash. They looked great, and we settled into a positive conversation. Finally, my people.

Shawn had been a hiking friend for years, so it was natural to have him there with Prakash. Seeing Prakash brought tears to my eyes. I extended my arm toward him, and he took my hand. He was my real-life hero. He was why I was sitting here, alive and breathing. How could I thank someone who had done such remarkable things for me? With tears, I tried thanking him multiple times, but Prakash stopped me in mid-sentence to thank me for being strong and not giving up. I had never met such a big-hearted person besides Chris. After a remarkable hour, I got another knock on the door.

Josh had gone home to spend some time with JB, and Prakash and Shawn would head out soon as well. I wasn't expecting any more visitors that evening. With a little anxiety, I asked, "Who is it?"

A deep voice came back. "It's your father."

I got a sick feeling in my stomach that almost activated my old vomit reflex. I pushed my dinner away. It was late. Why didn't anyone warn me he was coming? I couldn't handle my father when I was at the top of my game, let alone now. I was scared to answer. I wanted to bellow, "Go away."

*Breathe.* I tried to remain positive and thought that maybe he would be kind. *For once in his life, could he be happy that I was alive? Could he say one agreeable thing? Okay, Alyson, collect yourself.* I replied, "Come in."

My father opened the door. I introduced Shawn and Prakash and, with a swish of an invisible Darth Vader cape, the room immediately felt awkward. My dad was a champion at one thing. He could turn any joyful time into a time of misery. Prakash and Shawn tried to make small talk with my dad, but soon decided it was time for them to leave. I made plans with them for a future visit. Shawn and Prakash were the people I most wanted to see, and my dad had driven them away. As they headed for the door, I waved my goodbyes. After the door click, the silence was deafening.

After wiping my tears clear, I decided to break the silence. Looking him straight in the eye, I said, "Thanks for coming dad. I'm happy to be alive."

"You're lucky to be alive," he said. "You shouldn't have been there in the first place. Why do you think you need to go mountain climbing in the dead of winter anyway? How could you put your dog in that kind of danger? What if something happened to JB? I hope this is going to open your eyes. I hope you're over this stupid mountain climbing thing you've been stuck on."

Before he could say anything more about his notion of a real life, I said through the roaring silence, "Are you kidding me?"

Each stumbled word that came from his mouth was like a knife thrust into my heart. He couldn't stop. Jab after jab, deeper and deeper. Kill was his only verb. I understood that he never had a true passion. I understood that he never wanted children but ended up with five and resented us. I understood that he resented me because I was touched by the truth. I understood that it was my belief that if you had children, you wanted the best for them. I knew that a parent should share in their children's lives and their happiness.

Following my dad's example, I had become a drunken drug addict, but had changed my life into an ambitious college graduate.

I understood that I wasn't good enough for my dad. I understood that if I had ten kids, I wouldn't please my dad. I understood that if I won the Boston Marathon with a new world record, I would not please my dad. I understood that if I flapped my arms and flew to the Moon, I would not please my dad. I understood that, even in that case, he would put me down for not making it to Mars. It was time for the full truth.

The authentic Alyson stared at the strange man in the room. She let silence rumble around his ears. Feeling that she no longer needed a dad, she wiped a tear from her eye. For once, she let him become the uncomfortable one. Finally, the authentic Alyson spoke.

"Dad, whoever you are, I love you. I don't care if you care about that. Somewhere deep down inside, I think that you might love me. For some sick reason, you're unable to show it. I can no longer grieve over that. I cannot live my life to please you. If I had died on that mountain, you would always blame me for my own death. You have such a negative view of me, and it's all yours now. I can't hear your opinions any longer. I can't stand the negativity."

The "post-accident" Alyson let her words settle, then punctuated them with more silence. When it was clear that my father no longer had the last word, I continued, struggling not to cry.

"I want you to leave. I want you to leave now. I don't want to talk to you. If, by some miracle, you find it in your heart to accept me for the person I am, let me know, and perhaps we can start over and leave the past where it belongs—in the past."

Waving him toward the door with the back of my hand, I concluded, "I'm done. I can't deal with the pain you are causing me." Tears ran down my face. I knew this father belonged in my old life, my pre-accident life, my life of despair.

# Part Two

# On The Mend

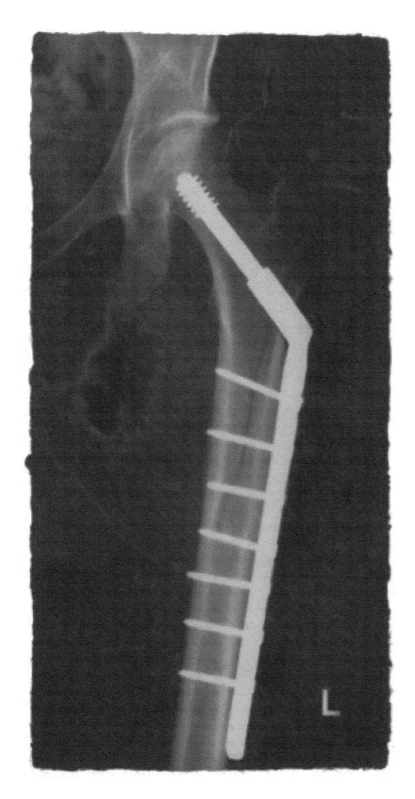

# Chapter 16 – Picking Up The Pieces

*Get me out of this hospital! I can't handle another night!*

Pain and bad dreams woke me so often that I thought I had lost my mind. Why would anyone wake you up to give you a sleeping pill? On the mountain, the thought of lying in a comfortable hospital bed kept me alive. Now that I was here, it wasn't pleasant. I lay immobile on my back and had pain from surgery. I was dosed with pain medications, but they came with side effects. My leg throbbed and I had too much time to think. My thoughts still swirled.

Spinning during the night, I focused on the fact that I was alive and would recover. My mind charged ahead, and I couldn't stop thinking about my second chance at life. I thought about the changes I had vowed to make on Rosalie Peak. While thoughts of a new life brought comfort, it also brought anxiety. New questions piled up. With a titanium rod in my leg, it was clear that I faced a long rehab period with no running and no mountains, and I felt trapped in my marriage.

They took me to Swedish Medical Center, a hospital that was a few miles from our house. I hated hospitals. Besides breaking an arm twice in high school, nothing serious had happened to me that required a hospital stay. This was new territory and I didn't like it. I needed help doing everything. I hope I never have that helpless feeling again. I also gained a new appreciation for nurses during my stay. Nurses are amazing human beings, and I wouldn't have gotten out of the hospital without their help, care, and encouragement.

Would I stick by everything that I promised myself on the mountain? Promises were easy. The road ahead would be difficult. I knew the accident was a turning point in my life, and that from this point forward I wouldn't cave in and let other people run the show. I would do whatever it took to fulfill the promises that I made on Rosalie.

On the mountain, I had a clear vision about what I needed to do. It seemed simple. I needed to end my marriage, overcome my eating disorder, find love, and live happily. I hoped that I could encourage and help others to have the courage and strength to break free from their pain. But being incapacitated and at the mercy of other people, I was in no position to do anything.

Before the accident on Rosalie, I had little self-confidence or belief in my abilities. I had survived the accident, but I asked myself if I was strong enough, brave enough, and determined enough to change my path. I felt that I couldn't talk to anyone in my family about my situation. I needed to find someone who would understand. I couldn't unload on acquaintances and I thought a therapist wouldn't be much help for my current state. It would take too long to explain my past and I was in a hurry to leave my old life behind.

I felt alone and tormented. I realized that I needed encouragement and love to heal my body and soul. I had cut ties to my previous life when I quit drinking and using drugs. I had removed myself from that crowd and started over with no peers to support me. Making changes would be the hardest part of my recovery. I was frightened knowing that I had to make this journey alone. As much as I wanted to change, I doubted that I was strong enough to make the changes. Still, I knew I was strong enough. My accident proved my strength. I knew after surviving what I had been through, I could do anything. I just needed to believe.

I wondered how long it would be like this. How long would I be a prisoner in a broken body? I was in a hurry and my lack of patience inevitably gave way to self-pity. I was sickened by the thought that my eating disorder had caused the accident. My poor bones. Would they ever recover? Who would have thought that binging and purging would weaken bones to the point of snapping? I never thought of that until it happened. How could I ever really tell anyone that I did this to myself? Now I would have an ugly scar on my leg to remind me. It would always be a reminder of Rosalie and the changes I vowed to make. My accident was the best and worst thing that ever happened to me. It made me see how precious life is and that your life could be over in the blink of an eye. My accident was the start of living life to the fullest and breaking free from a past that haunted me and my marriage.

Questions piled up. Would I give up climbing mountains since an accident almost killed me? My family didn't want me to climb, especially my dad. I knew that I could give in and stop climbing. I could start a family and follow the expected plan. They would be happy, but I would be miserable. I realized that I couldn't live a lie and had to be true to myself. If I was going to be "normal," I might as well have died on the mountain. I had to be me. Could I trade the loss of my husband and family to finally be myself? I knew that I had to do that, and hoped that they could understand and forgive me.

I dreaded leaving the hospital because that meant going home to face my new reality. I had made serious promises to myself and to God. In my deepest despair, I asked God to let me live and give me a second chance. The rest was up to me. The fact that I lay on a hospital bed with a throbbing leg and spinning thoughts was an answer. The authentic Alyson wanted to overcome the obstacles in my path to freedom.

The road ahead was a new mountain to climb, but I was different now. I had escaped death's grip, and now had to embrace a new life. Remembering the white light and transcendence toward heaven, I knew that I had almost died. I crashed back to the mountain for a reason. My second chance was not a random accident. It was a mission, and I had a responsibility to fulfill it. I had to believe in myself. I had to find a way to trust that I had made the right decision to change my path. I felt that if I could help one person to have a better life, then the emotional and physical pain would be worthwhile. But I had to make it first, and then I could make a difference.

## Home

I was in the hospital for almost a week. Returning home was my first challenge, then I would figure out work and the rest of my life. At the time of the accident, I owned a small business. I had a contractor working for me, and knew she would need to take over my accounts while I recovered. I also worked at FedEx in the evenings, and I was in a master's degree program at CU Denver.

Continuing online classes would be something I could do while recovering. It was important to finish my degree.

I left the hospital in a wheelchair. The ride home was interesting because I felt every bump and movement of the car. I wondered if the accident had made me super-sensitive to the surroundings or if it was pain. After the hospital discharged me, Josh took me home. He gathered my things from my week-long stay and loaded them into the car. I sat in a wheelchair and Josh pushed me to the car. Getting Josh to help me from the wheelchair into the Toyota 4Runner wasn't easy or pain free. As we drove away from the hospital, I stared out the window. An emptiness filled me. *Just remember to breathe.*

As the car pulled into the driveway, I faced another obstacle that I hadn't anticipated. After crutching toward the front door, I discovered the porch step now seemed tall and steep as I balanced on my crutches. *Would I put both crutches up first?* That didn't seem safe. *Would I leave both crutches down and balance on them while I went for it with my right foot?* I could fall backwards. Before I could choose, Josh helped me up the step. I felt ashamed for the pain I was going to cause him. He was kind and caring, and deserved better. He deserved happiness.

Flowers, cards, and stuffed animals crowded the entryway. Suddenly, my home felt welcoming and warm. There were so many stuffed animals that Josh had to move them out of the way so I could get to the living room. The struggle from the hospital to the car, the ride home, the walk to the front door, the climb up the steps, and the walk through the house had exhausted me. I collapsed on the sofa.

Obviously, people cared about me. Josh's family had reached out. Josh was attentive and that made it difficult to escape the thoughts about ending our marriage and its impact on him. I was medicated and I couldn't think about it too long. I couldn't focus on anything except getting comfortable on the couch. I was home and fell into a deep sleep.

# ED Redux

I was active before the accident, so being parked on the sofa was a dismal change. Everybody encouraged me and said it would get better, that I would recover. Everyone assumed that I was alert and rational enough to calmly accept their encouragements. But the pain medications kept me in a fog and no one knew the turmoil I was experiencing. *How would I survive inactivity for so long?* A miserable thought crept into my head. *Without exercise, I'm going to get fat.* My logical side knew that this was the old eating disorder voice working its evil magic, but my emotional side believed the voice. I pushed logic back to the front. *I don't want to get fat so I'll cut back on eating until I'm recovered. Does this eating disorder thing ever entirely go away? How am I going to control it?* If only the nasty thoughts of binging and enjoying it - and then purging so that I wouldn't gain weight - would just go away.

I knew that I couldn't return to binging and purging. The eating disorder had weakened my bones and nearly taken my life. The doctor's voice echoed in my head, and I knew that I could solve the eating disorder. Choosing to live with an eating disorder would be self-destructive and a death sentence. I thought about people who learn that they have only weeks to live. I thought that their remaining time would be so precious, and they would be disgusted by someone who chose to throw away their life. It was clear what I had to do.

The eating disorder voice was prominent in my head for years, and I hadn't been able to turn it off. I had stopped smoking, drinking, and using drugs by using will power, work ethic, and determination. It wasn't easy, but I did it. Silencing my ED voice proved to be my most difficult challenge.

Lying on the cold rock slab on Rosalie Peak, I figured out what fueled my ED voice - lack of confidence, low self-esteem and not living true to my convictions. It was a voice of doubt and weakness. I figured I had to dissolve my marriage, and then resolve the eating disorder.

I lay immobile on the sofa with caring Josh tending every need. There was no simple solution. I couldn't postpone the battle with my ED voice; I had to at least muzzle it for now.

I had to learn to accept who I am and be happy with that, and stop worrying about how others perceived me. *How would I do that?* I had to charge ahead with the plan for my new life and resist the temptation to give up. For so long I believed that I couldn't do much on my own, so it was difficult for me to think I could actually change my life. But I had to believe it - my life depended upon it. My accident changed me and now I had to change my life.

## On Drugs Again

The sofa was a place of pain even though I was medicated on oxycodone, a potent drug similar to morphine. My first few days at home were dulled by the drugs, but it was scary that my ED voice had pushed through the fog. Obviously, I couldn't divorce Josh tomorrow. But I couldn't just turn off my ED voice and I couldn't escape into oxycodone forever. Slab and sofa started to feel the same. My recovery needed to be broken into baby steps. One of the side effects of oxycodone is a loss of appetite. I thought that might quiet the ED voice for a while.

Even with drugs, the pain was so intense that I couldn't do anything on my own. Josh helped me with everything. My first shower was an ordeal. I didn't want to take another shower until I was completely healed. Getting up from the sofa to use the toilet was another heroic event. Instead of rocketing toward recovery, time slowed down, days became weeks. I couldn't think about the big picture and my next immediate need became my only concern.

Unfortunately, another side effect of oxycodone is constipation. After a week, I was in bad shape. The doctor explained that the solution was to stop taking the medication. I needed an intermediate baby step. With increasing abdominal pain, I used laxatives and stool softeners to get moving. I also knew that oxycodone could be habit-forming with regular doses. I felt that dependency coming on, so I knew that getting off the drug was a priority. I had to reduce it one step at a time. With my old dependency habits, this wasn't easy. I decreased my dose every day, which was tough because I was in pain. As I moved off the drug, I began thinking more clearly about my situation.

Sleep was also challenging. Since my first night at home, sleep was uncomfortable. I had terrible nightmares. In the dreams I was trapped on the mountainside, hearing the rescuers' muffled voices. My face was wrapped tightly in bits of clothing to protect me from the elements but I couldn't see anything. I could only hear the vague voices of the strangers trying to save my life. I was frozen in place and couldn't remove the clothing on my face to see or hear clearly. *What were they saying? Were they saying that it was too late? Were they saying that I was dead? Were they talking about leaving me, leaving me like the helicopter left me? Please don't go! I'm alive!* I would try to yell but my soundless mouth wouldn't move. Then I would wake up screaming and shivering, alive and terrified. As my heart pounded and my breath came in gasps, Josh calmed me down. It happened every night, so the doctor prescribed sleeping medication. He gave me another drug with other side effects, but fewer nightmares. The sleep medication helped, but using will power, I quickly reduced the dosage.

With less medication, my digestive system began behaving, and my mind was clearer. After a few weeks of recovery, I was in a better place. The support from family and friends was comforting, and the highlight of each day was having a visitor, which always cheered me up.

## Where are my Crutches?

My baby steps found crutches. Every day, I set a new walking distance goal. At first, I practiced in my room, then around the house. By the end of my first outside week, walking to the end of the street and turning around, I reached a distance of a half-mile. During crutch week two, I started laps around the neighborhood, increasing my distance. My friends, Jim and Cappy, visited often and helped my morale. As I progressed with my rehab mileage, they came in the morning and walked with me. I planned a three-mile park loop, but knew that this goal would require patience. With Jim and Cappy by my side, I knew I could do it.

Jim and Cappy motivated me every day to get outside and not get discouraged. I talked about my dreams with them on our daily walks. They offered positive encouragement, which I needed. Josh didn't walk with me often, since he worked most of the time. He worked at home, so he was able to care for me when I needed help. About six weeks after the accident, I saw real signs of recovery. The doctor told me that the femur, the biggest bone in the body, is the hardest and most painful bone to break. Fortunately, it's also the fastest to heal. Mountain climbing and running fantasies returned to my thoughts. I had become friends with Lynda from Search and Rescue. She was one of the first responders to reach me on Rosalie. I told her that I wanted to visit the Evergreen Search and Rescue facility to meet the team members and thank them for saving me. I especially wanted to thank a man named Tom who was instrumental in my successful rescue.

My sister agreed to drive me to a weekly meeting of the Search and Rescue teams. As I crutched into the facility, mixed emotions flooded over me. I looked around the room to see people rising to greet me and I felt welcome in their midst. I was overwhelmed by a deep feeling of gratitude. I wouldn't have survived without this organization. After the meeting began, I was asked to speak. Standing on my crutches, I told my story and thanked everyone for donating their time to help others. Members of the teams asked about the gear that helped save my life, about what went wrong, what went right, and what could be learned from my accident to help them in future rescues.

It brought me joy to answer their questions. I felt that I was taking the first step to help others. I also wanted to join a search and rescue team and help these selfless people save the lives of other victims. I wanted to be the person that told someone that she was going to make it. I wanted to say, "You're a survivor." I wanted my voice to be a life-line for someone to hang onto.

I met Tom, and choked back tears when I heard his familiar voice, thanking him profusely. Members of the team asked what had happened with the helicopter rescue.

I explained. I sat on the side of the mountain like a needle in a haystack. We saw the chopper but they didn't see us. It circled around the perimeter wasting time while the weather slowly deteriorated. Finally, they spotted me. The chopper landed and two nurses came toward me, but they were ill-prepared for the conditions. I think they thought I had a sprained ankle or something not as serious. Once they realized I needed a stretcher, they knew I wasn't going anywhere. They looked at me, looked at each other, and went back to the chopper. You could see the storm was about to hit us and there were only minutes before they would be trapped with me if they stayed. A moment later the helicopter took off. As they flew away, my thoughts of survival went with them. They left me nothing, not a sleeping bag, gear, or pain medicine. It was devastating, but I couldn't blame them.

Another member of the group spoke up, saying they should talk to the Flight for Life team and revisit their protocol for mountain rescues. If anything, I hoped that they learned something from my accident that would help them in the future. I left the meeting knowing that I was on the right path. Happiness filled my soul...

Prakash was also instrumental in saving my life. We became close after the accident. He visited me often at the hospital and at home. Had it not been for Prakash, I wouldn't have survived. He knew the right things to do in a bad situation and refused to let me slip away. I would be grateful forever for his caring and kind soul.

A month after the accident, Prakash received devastating news. His parents were in an automobile accident in India. His father had died, but his mother had survived. Prakash flew to India with his sister and brother to be with their family. Prakash's father had been a general surgeon and was, at age 72, still running 10-kilometer races three days a week. He performed surgeries, many for poor patients who couldn't afford medical care. Prakash's father was his idol. He was devastated by his father's death, and I felt helpless that I couldn't ease his sadness. As I grieved for Prakash, part of me felt comfort in knowing how much his father was loved.

After Prakash's tragedy, we didn't talk as frequently as I wanted. I thought that once we both had healed, time would allow us to be good friends again. Over the years, Prakash and I have remained friends. We didn't get out hiking, but the occasional BBQ did occur. Prakash married a beautiful woman and went on to have a stunning daughter. May she know one day how great her father is. Whether Prakash and I see each other or not, he will always be my hero and hold a special place in my heart.

I eventually worked up to three-mile park loops on my crutches. Every morning I saw an older woman who also walked around the park like I did. She was a delicate woman with wisps of silvery hair floating on the breeze. She used a cane, and couldn't move quickly. I made it my daily objective to beat the cane lady. That was a bit silly, but I needed a goal. The lady didn't seem to care or vary her pace. The day I finally passed her, she smiled as I crutched by and gave me a look that said, "Go for it, girl!" Her face was etched with lines formed by a lifetime of smiling. I couldn't help but admire her. She was an inspiration. She was living life her way.

With increased activity, my crutches began rubbing my armpits raw, so I went to the fabric store for extra padding. I didn't think that crutches could do that, but there were many things I didn't know about being disabled. I saw life through new eyes. Slowly, I appreciated all that I had been given. I was learning to give up focusing on things that couldn't be changed.

At this point, I wasn't eating much. My crutching wasn't much exercise compared to what I did before, and I battled with the ED voices warning me about getting fat. I needed to silence these voices and thought that I could use this down time to get serious help with my eating disorder. As a starting point, I looked for ED groups to join.

## Friends

Kevin Baker, whom I first met the morning of my accident, stayed in touch with me. He visited the hospital and introduced me to one of his friends, Teresa Gergen. Teresa, who had a similar accident to mine a year earlier, visited me in the hospital and offered to help me through my ordeal. She knew what lay ahead for my recovery and how tough it would be. I felt grateful for her help. Kevin came to my home a few times, and we made future plans to hike some easy trails.

Teresa also visited my home. Some mornings, she walked with me as I crutched and told me about her accident—a horrific ordeal—the rescue, and her recovery. Her story was similar to mine since she had broken her leg on a remote mountain. She survived the night with support from her teammates, and was rescued the next day. I felt a bond with Teresa from the moment we met. We had been through similar misfortunes so we understood one another.

I didn't know at the time that Teresa was a unique person. She was older and shorter than me, with long gray hair, glasses, a soft voice, and worked as a librarian. She would never strike you as a hardcore mountain climber. I later learned that she was the only woman to have climbed all of the 1,313 ranked peaks over 12,000 feet in Colorado. That's all of Colorado's Fourteeners, Thirteeners, and Twelvers—every peak in the state over twelve thousand feet. Later, she ascended the Eleveners and Teners to become the only person to have climbed the 2,311 ranked peaks over ten thousand feet in Colorado. Little did I know that I was walking in the morning with a peakbagging legend.

Alyson with Teresa Gergen on a local hike

Again, I was astounded by the hiking and climbing community. These people lived their passions and helped others to live theirs. This gave me strength. I wanted to be like them. I wanted to climb and run, and I wanted to help others understand that they deserve happiness. These people shared their experiences, words of encouragement, smiles, and nods of approval, helping others fulfill their dreams. I could no longer settle for being on the outside looking in. I wanted to encourage others to follow their dreams, embrace their passions, and learn to love themselves.

Teresa visited me one evening, and showed me the website listsofjohn.com. I had no idea how many 13,000- and 12,000-foot mountains were in Colorado, and that people strived to climb all of these peaks. I thought that finishing the Fourteeners was a huge deal, and the pinnacle of mountaineering accomplishment. It is a worthy achievement, but I discovered that the list of Fourteeners just scratched the surface of mountain difficulty, intensity, and beauty. It was overwhelming to discover all the peaks that other people climbed. I had been stuck hiking the same peaks because I didn't have a resource to provide information about other mountains. This incredible website was the key to hiking more peaks. A new mountain climbing door began opening for me.

I wondered what I did for so long without this valuable tool. I'm obsessive about things I do, so exploring the site's maps, lists, and reports fed my new appetite. Climbing all of Colorado's Thirteeners sounded like an amazing goal, since there are 584 ranked Thirteeners compared to 53 ranked Fourteeners. This was just the kind of goal that I yearned to complete. I had already climbed some of the highest Thirteeners, including many on the list of Colorado's 100 highest peaks. The 100 highest, or Centennial peak list, was another obvious goal. The possibilities were thrilling.

After reading about Colorado's mountains, I realized that many Thirteeners were tougher than the Fourteeners. Most had no trail to the summit, so climbing these remote peaks required navigational skills. Some Thirteeners were technical climbs that required ropes and rock-climbing equipment. One of the hardest is 13,113-foot Lizard Head, a sharp peak in the San Juan Mountains that was first climbed by Albert Ellingwood and Barton Hoag in 1921. I saw a photo of the peak and it looked impossible. I didn't know if I would ever be a good enough rock climber to reach the top of Lizard Head, but there are still hundreds of high peaks I could do on my own.

After an afternoon walk with Teresa, we spent a long session on listsofjohn. I surged with excitement about the future. I had to get through my recovery and start hiking again. The accident was in February, and I projected that I could be hiking up easy peaks by summer.

I enjoyed my friendship with Teresa and was ecstatic to be around someone who shared my passions. Teresa gave me a list of easy peaks that she had climbed after her accident. You could almost drive up some of these peaks, which was fine since I was in baby step mode. Even if a peak was easy and required little effort, I could log my ascent on listsofjohn.com which I found satisfying. It was inspiring to look at the site every day and see dozens of people bagging peaks. I hoped that one day I would meet these people and develop new friendships.

On one of our walks, I asked Teresa who was behind listsofjohn.com. Teresa told me that it was a guy, not surprisingly, named John. She knew John Kirk and had hiked with him before. She said that he was an incredibly fast hiker who had climbed a huge number of peaks. This sparked my interest, and I wondered if I would ever meet this John character. He sounded out of control like me - just the sort of person I wanted to meet.

During a peak discussion with Teresa, I asked her what she thought was the hardest high peak to climb in Colorado. She simply said, "Turret Ridge." She said that at 12,260 feet, it's the hardest obstacle that climbers finishing the list of 12,000-foot peaks must climb. She described tricky rock climbing up crumbling walls composed of rotten volcanic tuff, and that few people had successfully reached its summit. She told me about her ascent of Turret Ridge, noting steep walls and exposure, a place where only an eagle would feel at home. I thought to myself that I was thankful that it wasn't on my lists of prospective peaks.

While my head was filled with dreams and plans of future expeditions, I was unable to drive a car, so I walked a mile each way on crutches to my doctor's appointments. I did physical therapy sessions twice a week and a host of exercises that I had never tried. As my body healed, time sped up. During my recovery, I was carefully picking up the scattered pieces of my life and moving toward a new future.

Alyson and JB

# Chapter 17 – A Paradox

I told Josh about the Colorado Thirteeners, how many there were, and how many people had climbed them all. I told him about listsofjohn and how excited I was to climb peaks listed there. Josh hadn't finished hiking the Fourteeners and had no desire to consider a list like the Thirteeners. He eventually finished the Fourteeners and said they had nearly killed him. Even when we climbed together, he complained about the early starts and long drives. But I liked the new information that I learned about the thousands of other Colorado peaks. It was like a gift under the Christmas tree; a gift of beauty, adventure, and summits.

Josh couldn't believe that I wanted to climb more mountains after what had just happened to me. I felt that he didn't get me. I wasn't afraid of climbing mountains because of the accident. Instead I viewed the accident as an eye opener and a blessing. It was the eating disorder, not the mountain, which almost took my life. The eating disorder was now fueled by my unhappy marriage, lack of self-esteem, and living a "fake" life. I realized that it was going to be difficult to implement my new plans, but felt this was the beginning of my journey. My promises on the mountain weren't a joke.

My heart knew that my time with Josh was limited. I felt guilty staying married and was sorry that Josh didn't know that I wanted to end it. I wasn't able to tell him that I wanted a divorce. My procrastination didn't help either of us. If Josh had only cheated on me, or done something despicable, I could feel justified in leaving him. Instead, I was trying to justify what seemed like a selfish act to be free. Often, I found myself wondering how many people go through this ordeal in their lives. I watched my mother live thirty-plus years in an unhappy marriage. Why do people go through life unhappy? The answer to me was obvious. Sometimes when we are conditioned to live a certain way, change is scary. Living authentically is scary. Hurting someone you care about is scary. The question was, would I let fear win?

March and April crept by. The extra padding on the crutch armpits wore out, and I was ready to be off the crutches. Work was covered since I had a leave of absence from FedEx, and the contractor covered my small business. I wasn't sure when I could work again and didn't plan until I figured out the next moves in my life. I knew what I had to do, but didn't know how to get there.

I also decided to write a book about my ordeal. I figured that I would write down what happened to me and what I had learned from the accident. The book also could help others trapped in similar cycles of self-destruction and despair. I wanted, of course, to have a happy ending, but there wasn't one yet. I had to find a way to stop the self-doubt and self-destructive behaviors. I knew I had serious things to overcome and I had to face down my eating disorder.

A huge life accomplishment for me was to quit smoking, drinking, and doing drugs. Drugs and alcohol had helped me escape from life. I knew they were dangerous, but the escapes were so delicious. I couldn't stop until I had a good reason. One day, I wondered why I couldn't quit. It wasn't that easy. I had to discover why my life was so bad that I had to escape from it. I didn't like the person I had become and wanted to escape from myself and all the bad things in my life. I knew that I did things because my friends did them. I wanted to be liked and accepted. I also knew that my father's rejection drove me to seek acceptance and approval from my friends who eagerly encouraged each other with unhealthy habits.

As I understood why I used drugs, drank alcohol, and smoked cigarettes, I began thinking of them as demons trying to control me. It wasn't easy to break free of the demons. I had to give up friendships, find different hangouts, and find a new career path. My mom and dad continued to drink and smoke, but that was different. I disliked their self-destructive behaviors and wanted to get away from them.

At the time, I liked my friends and hated that I had to get away from them. In seeking change, I knew that I couldn't be around them while I was trying to quit. I needed to stop hanging out with friends that were a bad influence. Unfortunately, this did not leave me many friends. I felt alone as I began this change.

Eventually, I managed to quit smoking, drinking, and drugs, but the cost was losing my friends, a painful trade-off, but one I would do again in a heartbeat.

Almost everyone who tries to quit their vices uses substitutes like chewing gum, ice cream, or candy as a reward for giving up the bad stuff. For me, the reward was running and climbing without struggling for breath or fighting a hangover. Other rewards were peace and serenity on mountain tops and the thrill of running a trail. The runner's high and the adrenaline rush were new addictions, but not destructive ones. They made me feel alive.

Kevin Baker came to my house for a few barbecues in April. One time, he visited after climbing and commented on how well I was recovering. I told him that I would be up in no time, and that I had the new goal of climbing all the Thirteeners. He said that he was already climbing that list and that we could do some together when I was ready. He also offered to climb some low peaks with me to get ready for the Thirteeners when I was off the crutches. This mountain talk made me want to pitch the crutches, dive out the window, and sprint toward the mountains.

Leaving my marriage and perhaps finding a soul-mate dominated my thoughts. Josh was a good person and treated me well. If I stayed with him I could be "just fine" and make everyone happy. How could I abandon such a good person? The better question was: *Why was I unhappy?* The answer was that I just knew that I married the wrong person. I had settled and knew it.

Was someone out there who liked climbing peaks and finding adventure like I did? If I threw away my current life for the unknown, would I regret my decision? If I left Josh, would my family forgive me? My brothers, sister, and parents liked Josh. My mom had talked me out of calling off the wedding. My little brother Dan and Josh were solid friends. Many people besides Josh and me would be affected if I left him. The breakup would clearly be harder than I had imagined, but it was my life and I was unhappy. I had to make these hard decisions for myself. Knowing that people would be hurt made doing it that much harder. I put off the inevitable.

# Fruita

In November 2010, a few months before my accident, Josh and I visited the town of Fruita on Colorado's western slope. I had signed up to run a marathon through nearby Colorado National Monument and Josh went with me to check out the area. He planned to drive through the monument and wait for me at the finish line. The marathon course was loaded with canyon vistas dotted with sandstone towers. This area is quite different from Colorado's mountains, and Josh loved Fruita. After the trip, Josh talked about moving to Fruita someday. It was possible, since Josh worked from home and could live anywhere. I could restart my business and transfer my FedEx job. We could make it happen.

The idea of moving to Fruita was terrifying. It's was a five-hour drive from our Denver-area home. I lived only twenty minutes from my family, and a move to Fruita would create a significant separation. More importantly, knowing the promises I had made, I didn't want to move there. I struggled with my decision, wondering if maybe moving to Fruita would allow Josh to reconnect with the outdoors. This didn't seem likely, but I didn't have much else to hope for.

During my recovery, Josh pushed hard to move to Fruita. We drove there on several spring weekends and looked at houses. The idea of moving across the state with a man I was going to divorce confused me, I was afraid that I was taking a drastic action before I could touch my new vision. I needed help, someone to guide me, since I didn't trust in myself.

Adding to my misery, I also loved the area. There were many trails and new peaks to climb, plus Fruita was close to the San Juan Range and its hundreds of Thirteeners. I slowly began to accept the idea of moving to Fruita. I decided that if I moved, I would pursue my Thirteener goal whether he joined me or not. This thought both scared and excited me.

Going back and forth on my promises to myself, I felt that I needed to give our marriage another chance so I agreed to move to Fruita. I contacted the Mesa County Search and Rescue Team and learned the requirements for becoming a member. Speaking with the team's leader, I learned about the group. I explained my

165

accident and rescue and the leader understood why I wanted to join SAR. He said I would make a great addition and couldn't wait for me to join. I filled out an application and once it was approved, I would be a part of a team that had helped to save lives. I had to give it a chance.

## April Showers Bring May Flowers

After two months of recovery, I began healing faster. I began walking without crutches, only using them on longer outings, since my left leg became weak after a few miles. Kevin and I hiked up some easy peaks close to Denver. We started with 6,855-foot Green Mountain in Lakewood, a suburb in west Denver. This urban peak provided a three-mile hike on a good trail. The hike seemed easy, but I was afraid it would be painful and difficult. After being cooped up for months, it was great getting outside with Kevin, a solid hiking partner.

The next week, I tackled 6,575-foot North Table Mountain, an easy peak in Golden. We hiked up the wide trail onto a broad plateau, but the rocky summit of North Table looked difficult. Kevin said it wasn't hard, and that I would be fine. Focusing on the last section, I crutched over to the base of the summit rocks. I didn't trust my leg to step up so I stuck with the crutches and carefully climbed the last 50 feet to the top. I was shaky, but I wasn't a normal hiker and, for the first time in months, I felt like a climber.

Kevin took photos of me with my phone camera. I was excited to do more than a simple walkup, so I sent pictures to a few family members. I got back negative responses. My family wasn't amused by my ascent and didn't want to hear that I had recovered enough to climb again. They didn't understand that I needed a challenge and that I found peace on mountaintops.

While Kevin encouraged me to do what I loved, Josh wanted me to quit hiking. This made me sad and scared, and my feelings about ending my marriage grew stronger. I knew that I couldn't end it easily. I felt conflicted and didn't know how to escape without hurting others. If I made the wrong choices, they would be hard to fix. I knew in my heart that I needed a divorce, but I didn't trust my instincts so I waffled between going and staying.

Kevin was a wonderful person and good hiking partner, and I needed more people like him in my life. We made peakbagging plans for the upcoming summer, planning to climb some Thirteeners. Josh met Kevin at a family barbecue and they seemed to like each other. Most of my friends were men, so introducing Kevin to Josh was an ordinary event.

## No Means Yes

Doctor's orders are supposed to be obeyed, but sometimes, when a doctor tells me no, I take it to mean yes. I wanted to run a race in the summer to prove that I had recovered and to have a training goal. I needed a spark of excitement in my life. On a regular checkup with my doctor, I told him that I wanted to run a marathon that summer. He folded his hands and politely told me that I was crazy, then launched into a lecture why I shouldn't run a marathon. He said I should lower my expectations. I reached for my phone to show him pictures of me crutching up North Table Mountain but when I looked up, he was heading for the door.

When people tell me that I can't do something, it drives me crazy and only makes me want to do it just to prove that I can. I hurried home and looked at my running websites. To hell with a marathon, I found a race that sparked my interest, the Grand Mesa 50-Miler. Maybe I was crazy to think about running a 50-mile race only five months after breaking my femur.

By conventional standards, I was out of my mind, but I also knew that if I could survive Rosalie, then anything was possible. I had stayed in touch with Lynda, the woman who was one of the first responders to reach me on Rosalie. She and her boyfriend came over for dinner in May and I got to know her better. Lynda and I clicked, since she understood my adventure passion. She had her own passions, like climbing mountains and running100-mile races. The thought of running 100 miles seemed absurd, but I also thought that maybe one day I would try the distance.

167

During my rescue, Lynda had talked about the Leadville 100, which was a tantalizing distraction that nudged my mind off the pain. I remembered that conversation and asked Lynda if she was going to run Leadville in August. She said yes, and that she was training hard to get under a 25-hour finish. Without thinking, I asked, "Lynda, can I pace you at Leadville like we talked about during my rescue? I'll be ready. I'm registered for a 50-miler in July!"

She was blown away, but she knew I was ambitious and ready to get back on my feet. Lynda thought for a moment, and said, "Absolutely!" That was it. I would work my butt off and pace my rescuer in the Leadville 100. I was so excited.

It was painful, but I started driving again in mid-May. This was a big step, since it was annoying to rely on others to drive me around. Getting in and out of the car was difficult but this was my ticket to freedom. The accident made me realize that we never know how long we will have the opportunity to see our loved ones. So, I began visiting my family often. I wasn't working, school had ended for the semester, and I had plenty of free time.

## Dream Home or Dreaming?

Josh finally found his dream home in Fruita that spring and we drove out to see it. The beautiful house was brand new. Josh made the decision that we were moving and, even though I didn't know how to feel or react, I was in no position to fight his decision. I was confused by the trauma of the past few months and my promises. Part of me hoped that being away from my family would help us grow closer and that maybe Josh would love hiking again. I supported Josh. We were moving to Fruita.

Reality pursued a different dream. As summer approached, I grew close to Kevin and slid away from Josh. Kevin was a good friend and hiking partner. With Josh came JB, and I loved that sweet dog. The thought of losing him was torture.

Josh and I put an offer on the Fruita house, it was accepted, and we planned to move in late July. That gave me two months to make big decisions. I knew what the right thing to do was, but I hated hurting people. When I found quiet time, the voice of my old friend Chris told me what to do. It was time for Alyson to take care of Alyson. I needed quality mountain time to clear my head and chart my course.

## Internal Healing

The need to heal internally was critical to cure my eating disorder. To get help with this process, I went to an eating disorder seminar. It helped to meet other people sharing the same struggles. I was not alone.

Since I booted him from my hospital room, my dad hadn't been to see me. Even though the way we left things at the hospital was awful, I didn't want to interact with him. I had spent decades trying to fix our relationship and mend every problem. I felt the tug of that old pattern, but I couldn't afford to care anymore. I wasn't going to call him, yet. I discarded my old addictions without dealing with the root reasons that I used to escape into them. My relationship with my father was something that hurt me and I knew that I had to come to terms with it to heal myself.

It took time, but my dad eventually called Josh to see how I was doing. I was upset that he didn't call me. After a month of this two-step, I decided to ask my dad to go to therapy with me. The eating disorder specialist from the group sessions also did individual therapy, so I arranged to start therapy together, and my dad agreed to go. That told me that he wanted to have a relationship with me. Maybe some professional help could mend the wounds from our past relationship. At a minimum, it would expose our problems. Perhaps the wounds were fatal, but I was going to try anyway. I couldn't articulate why, but I wanted my father to love me and be proud of me.

The therapy sessions were intense. We had to go deep into our pasts, and I had to revisit many childhood events. In the safety of therapy, I told my dad about things that he did but possibly did not remember because he was intoxicated. I told him that one incident gave me nightmares for months, dreaming that he had killed my mother. He didn't deny these things and I felt a huge weight come off my shoulders. There was a glimmer that I had a chance at a real father-daughter relationship.

The therapist walked us through a process of taking the bad stuff and putting it into a box, then taking that box and disposing of it however we felt best. We could blow it up, throw it off a cliff, or bury it, but we had to let go of the past and move toward the future. This visualization was good, but would it be good enough? It is much easier said than done. There is much healing that must happen before the pains of the past can be thrown out and never revisited.

Between my recovery, Josh dilemma, eating disorder, and family pressures, it felt like the world was against me. All I had to support me was my passion and a dream. My life was twisting into a huge knot, and it started to look like I might have to cut my way out. With June busting out, I tried to forget my life's mess and followed my feet to the mountains.


## Bartlett Mountain

Kevin and I planned to climb some high Thirteeners. He wanted to scramble up Bartlett Mountain in Lake County. It was an easy peak for the most part, but the problem was that the Climax Molybdenum mine had whacked away at the peak's west face, taking over 150 feet off the top. The remaining crest was a jagged remnant. The peak offered hefty scrambling, and reports indicated that the summit pinnacle was rotten and a fall would likely be fatal. Bartlett wasn't a good Thirteener for me to climb after my recovery, but I was up for the challenge. Of course, I said nothing to my family. My left leg was weaker than my right, but only training would strengthen my left leg.

I saw photos of the mountain and became nervous. The summit's loose rock looked frightening. Kevin invited Heather, another climber, on the hike, so we became a team of three. Heather was a rock climber, peakbagger, and runner. She was easy-going, so we clicked right away.

We headed up Bartlett on Sunday, June 12. Worrying about the scramble at the rocky summit distracted me from lower snow slopes that we had to cross. Snow had caused my fall on Rosalie, and with the snow came fear I didn't know I had. A fall on my first peak after recovery was unthinkable, but possible. Kevin kicked bucket-sized steps, and I crept after him with my gimpy left leg. I stayed focused and didn't let fear overcome me.

We finally reached the shaky traverse near the mountain top. It was worse than the photo I saw in the comfort of my home. The summit spire, surrounded by crumbling rock, looked ridiculous. I didn't think I could do it, but the summit register dangled tantalizingly from the uppermost spire. I summoned my strength, took a deep breath, and resolved to make it. I told myself that it wasn't the mountain challenging me, it was me challenging myself.

Kevin went first, traversing to the spire, and climbing it. I watched with awe. Heather said she would stay close to me and help me across the scary moves up the summit spire. She started, and I followed. We inched over to the tower base, and I crept up the summit spire. When I touched the top and peered down the steeper backside, I wondered if the entire summit could crumble into the abyss with me on it. This was the most unnerved I'd ever felt on a peak. I crept back to safer terrain and suddenly felt more alive than ever. The danger and excitement stirred me.

After Bartlett, Kevin and I discussed more plans. Many of the peaks we wanted to climb required long drives, so I began taking off for three or four days at a time on hiking trips. I felt a new outlook on life with my goal of climbing the Thirteeners. The more peaks I climbed with Kevin, the more I knew that life with Josh needed to end. I had to build up the courage to end the marriage, tell my family, and end the long charade. By this point, I was tired of hearing myself say I needed to leave Josh.

## The Castle

I had more courage to try harder peaks when I climbed with Kevin. He could lead mountains that required ropes, and I continued to learn technical climbing skills. At the end of June, Kevin invited me to climb a 9,691-foot peak called the Castle, a technical Class 5.4 climb that required ropes and climbing gear. It would be my hardest peak, but I was up for it.

We headed up to the Castle on Monday, June 27. Some of the climbing was scary, but being belayed on a rope from above made me feel safe. The final pitch to the summit was intense. After watching Kevin climb, I wasn't sure I could do it, but I would never know until I tried. After struggling to keep my fears in check and a lot of grunting, it wasn't long until I sat on the summit soaking in the views. I felt alive and wanted to do more rock climbing.

## Grand Endeavor

The Grand Mesa 50-mile ultra-marathon was set for Saturday, July 23. My new friend Heather was also running the 50-miler and, since it was her first "50," I hoped that we would have similar speeds. I reached Grand Mesa before Heather and, checking on listsofjohn, discovered that Grand Mesa offered many peaks. When Heather arrived, we decided to climb Leon Peak, the highest point in Mesa County, the evening before the race as a warm up. That night we camped near the race's starting line.

The next morning, I met the race director, Phil Berghauser, and told him about my accident, limitations, and how nervous I was. Phil said that I could drop out at any aid station and get a ride back to the starting line. With this comforting news, I knew that I had nothing to lose. If my leg acted up or if the run became too painful, I could stop. I was in control.

We ran along a narrow ridge for the first ten miles and reached the top of Crag Crest. At mile 25, I was okay, but began struggling during the last 25 miles. My thigh ached, and the pain increased with each mile. For the last ten miles, it felt like someone was pounding on my left leg with a hammer. I was now a pain pro, but I didn't know if I could keep running. Worse, I was scared that I wouldn't be able to run anymore. I dug deep and told myself that the pain wasn't as bad as what I'd endured on Rosalie, and that it would end at the finish line.

Despite all the doctor's speeches that I was out of my mind, I crossed the finish line with Heather in a time of 12:59. Five months after my accident, my Grand Mesa 50 was a success. This was my first trip to Grand Mesa, and I knew that I would be back. I didn't know that Colorado had so many beautiful wildflowers, and the Mesa harbored more lakes than I imagined were in the entire state. Surrounded by beauty, my heart felt at peace and my mind at ease.

The Grand Mesa race series also has a 100-mile race. On the surface, I thought that running 100 miles was outrageous, but I knew that one day I would take a 100-mile running journey. I would manage my leg pain and continue training. My friend Chris had always talked about running the Leadville 100. One day, I would run that race in his honor.

## Decisions

After the Grand Mesa 50, I battled with myself about doing the "right thing." I was raised Catholic and divorce wasn't an option. You got married and made it work. You took vows when you got married that were for better or worse. I drove an hour and a half to Fruita to stay with Josh and to see how I felt about the new home.

As I drove I asked myself if maybe the Western Slope would grow on me. If I decided to move and give my marriage a second chance, could we make it work? My gut told me that I didn't have any right to expect Josh to change who he was any more than he had the right to change who I was. The feeling that times had changed and people grow apart and make mistakes was apparent, being raised Catholic was no reason to stay. In the past few months since my awakening on Rosalie, what kind of a marriage did we have when I was absent much of the time? And why didn't Josh want to be with me in the mountains like we were at the beginning?

I had avoided Josh for the first half of the summer. He knew something was wrong. He probably blamed my change on the accident and believed I would straighten out. I didn't know if I was his soul-mate or if I would break his heart with a divorce. With our differences, staying married to me would cheat Josh out of a life filled with love and companionship. That sounded worse to me.

We closed on the Fruita house in late July, and Josh planned to move right away. We had renters lined up for our Denver home for August 1, but I wasn't preparing to move with Josh. I was supposed to find someone to take over my business in Denver and get a transfer to the Western Slope with FedEx. I had simply chosen not to have time for these things, since I was busy climbing peaks. I told Josh that I wasn't having any luck with either job issue, and that I needed more time before moving. I kept procrastinating. Josh understood, and said that I should stay with my parents until I was ready. At this point, my dad and I were in the best place we had ever been and I didn't have many options, so moving in with my family seemed reasonable.

We packed up the Denver house and moved a mountain of stuff to Fruita. My Denver life was over and a new life in Fruita awaited me. The Fruita house was in a quiet, peaceful neighborhood. There were views in every direction and trails were minutes away. My thoughts bounced from my life with Josh, the known life, the "just fine" life, and the unknown life I had promised myself. Was I going to toss a decade with Josh for a life of uncertainty, problems, and possible failure? My battered body continued to heal, but my eating disorder voice gnawed at me. In the silence of the nights, I could think clearly, and I knew that somehow, I would spring free.

Life changes are tough. I was scared of the changes facing me, but my eating disorder made me sicker. I had to get control over it. Moving into my parent's home was weird, since I hadn't lived there for many years. Now, at age 28, I was moving back with my parents. I also learned that my left quadriceps was half the size of my right one. I continued working with physical therapists to get full strength back. Since Josh now lived in Fruita, it was easier for me to go climbing. Kevin was unemployed at the time, so he was always available for mountain adventures.

My decision to leave Josh was made harder whenever I thought about losing JB. He was my dog, best friend, and my boy for years. We ran every morning and hiked every weekend. He felt like my child. One of my favorite moments with JB was when I gathered my hiking gear. He would run around the house because he knew that he'd soon be out in the woods. He loved the outdoors as much as I did. But JB was Josh's dog, not mine. I knew that keeping him would be impossible. When Josh moved to Fruita, he took JB with him. I didn't miss Josh, but I felt sharp pangs for my boy. I couldn't visualize never seeing JB again. It was tough, but I began taking baby steps to release my love for JB. I would always love JB, but I needed to learn how to let go. I couldn't stay married to Josh just to keep JB.

JB

# Chapter 18 – Cutting My Knot

Kevin liked group hikes, so he planned a trip to climb a few Elk Range Thirteeners near Aspen with some friends in early August. I told him that I would be there. We planned to meet at the Cathedral Lake Trailhead and climb Malemute Peak and two other peaks. We would camp at the trailhead on Friday evening and then start hiking at 4:30 a.m. on Saturday morning to get ahead of bad weather that might develop later in the day.

I didn't know several people that Kevin had invited, including John Kirk, the founder of the listsofjohn website. I was excited to meet the mastermind and, remembering what Teresa told me about him, he was apparently as obsessive about climbing peaks as me. Kevin told me that John was going through a divorce. The day before our meet up, Kevin and John climbed some peaks in the area. Kevin was also recently divorced and understood the difficulties involved in his struggle.

Arriving at the trailhead late Friday evening, I parked near Kevin's 4Runner, set up my bed, and tried to sleep for a few hours. My alarm beeped at 4:00 a.m. and I was ready to go in twenty minutes. The gang gathered around the trailhead with headlamps flashing into the dark. I grabbed my pack and scooted over to say hello. Kevin introduced me to the group. I met John and Renata Collard, a fit-looking couple. A tall man emerged from the shadows, and Kevin introduced me to John Kirk. When I looked at John, my headlamp blasted in his face. I apologized and shook his hand. My first view of John's face surprised me.

Kevin had told me that John was a nerd who was always on the computer doing technical stuff. From that description, I expected John to be much older and nerdier. My first glance told me that he was handsome, and had an amazing smile. He was the opposite of what I expected.

# Soul-mate

Soul-mate is a tricky word, perhaps the stuff of fairy tales. It's hard enough to figure out our own soul and even harder to find a mate for it. Everyone wants a soul-mate, but the search is complicated by life and the dream slips away like a childhood fantasy of a knight in shining armor. It's easy to profess undying love, but inevitable complications send dreams flying. In spite of my predicament, currently being married to Josh and having my life in chaos, I was hanging on to my dream. The rush of butterflies in my stomach told me that meeting John was about to change my life.

Our group set a strong pace up the hill, but we were comfortable enough to hold conversations. I chatted with the Collards, and then Kevin, and I caught up on everyone's past week's adventures. In the daylight, I could really see John. When he saw me behind him, he gave me a smile. He was no nerd. Well, there must be a nerd in there somewhere, I thought, since he had created the website that I loved. His blue eyes were intoxicating. Anyway, this nerd was a fast-hiking peakbagger extraordinaire. While hiking that day, John and I shared bits of our life stories.

I told John about my accident, my recovery, my quandary with moving to Fruita, and the fact that I wanted a divorce. John was impressed that I was climbing so well so soon, and I think he saw the passionate peakbagger inside me.

John shared his story and current situation. He met a woman years earlier when they were both into drinking. They stayed together, eventually marrying in Las Vegas - at the urging of others. John evolved during his marriage. He used to be an alcoholic and drug user like myself, but he quit on his own. During his marriage, he started climbing peaks more frequently for a healthier lifestyle.

We discovered that both of our spouses complained that we didn't drink. Our personalities wouldn't allow us to even have one drink. John was the first person I had met who understood this and overcame it like I did. John's wife had dealt him a worse hand than I held. I had brought my situation upon myself, but John still understood that it's almost impossible to be married to someone who doesn't share or understand your passions.

The group summited craggy Malemute Peak, and we gazed southwest at Castle Peak, the highest mountain in the Elk Range. Next up was Leahy Peak and then "Electric Pass Peak." John pointed out a gnarly traverse of five 13,000-foot peaks to the west that he was planning to hike as a day trip. Duh…I need to do that too! For today's loop, there was one mountain to go - an unnamed 12,060-foot peak. During the descent back to the trailhead, John and I zipped ahead and revealed more about ourselves. I found it easy to speak honestly about my life with him. As much as I wanted John to like me, I wasn't going to fake anything. We definitely communicated in an open-book style.

There was something about John that I didn't understand. In my life, I had never felt this mystified by anyone. We had just met and hardly knew each other. We pushed our guilt aside, hiked out together, and the guilty feelings passed. I didn't want it to be over.

Like a kid with a crush, I hoped to see John again. Back at the cars, we loaded our packs and changed into sandals. John and I exchanged phone numbers. I confided to him that I was supposed to go to Fruita that evening to reconcile my marriage, but I really didn't want to go. He said that if I ever wanted to hike and get some more Thirteeners, to give a call or text.

With my curiosity raging, I wanted to stay and hike with John the next day. I figured my marriage was over, so I didn't have to pretend. I said goodbyes to everyone, and when I shook hands with John, I held his hand longer than I should have. Then I headed west to Fruita - and Josh. When I reached Aspen, I pulled over, turned my phone on, and checked my messages and texts. I had several from Josh that ranged from angry to obnoxious. It sounded like he'd reached his own tipping point. I called him and the conversation disintegrated into a shouting match. Finally, after I had had enough, I hung up on him.

After the call, I was frustrated, upset, and shaking, and I didn't want to go to Fruita. I knew that Josh thought I was moving with him, but I had been a coward and let too much time pass. I should have told him months earlier before I came home from the hospital, "I love you, but I'm not in love with you, and I want a divorce." My actions may have said that but, if I'd been honest from the beginning, I would have saved a lot of time, money, energy, and emotion. The reason for this pain was my cowardice. I was a coward who made matters worse by not telling the truth and by letting this drag on.

I had reached the end of my rope and was ready to let go. I called John, and told him that I was staying in town and ready to do more peaks. We met at Subway and grabbed a sandwich. There were two smaller peaks nearby. I had climbed one the day before and John had done the other. So, I suggested that we show each other the other peak they hadn't done.

Walking up Red Hill, my phone constantly buzzed. Josh must have called my dad, because he was blowing up my phone with text messages. My dad was the last person I needed to have mad at me right now. I didn't want to deal with him. This was between Josh and me.

We talked about all the craziness that we were going through as we hiked. By the time we climbed Red Hill, I was so angry with Josh and my dad that I decided to head over to Fruita that evening. I wanted to stay with John and hike with him the following day, but I knew that I had to see Josh and tell him to his face that I didn't love him and wanted a divorce. After months of building up, the moment was finally here. It was time and there was no escaping now. Some people might be able to ask for a divorce with an email or text, but I wasn't going to do that. John and I hiked down Red Butte and then said our goodbyes.

It was difficult saying goodbye to John. I wanted to stay. I was drawn to John with an emotion that was stronger than anything I'd felt before. I wondered if he felt the same way. I told him that we should stay in touch and plan another hike soon.

## Saying Goodbye

It's never easy to hurt someone you care about. In Fruita, Josh and I talked that night, but he had a different agenda. That was the last time we were intimate. I was glad it happened because it confirmed everything I already knew. There was nothing left between us, and after the act was over I knew our marriage was finished.

We got up the next day and went hiking. It was good to see JB. I loved that dog and, to be honest, I felt closer to JB than Josh. On the hike, I told Josh about my feelings as openly as I could without being hurtful. I said that during our decade together we had both changed, and that I decided not to move to Fruita. I tried to explain that I wanted to be married to someone that I was head over heels in love with and shared the same passions. He heard the words, and I think he understood, but I knew he hurt. It made me sad to put him through this.

After that visit, I felt that a huge weight was lifted off my shoulders. Maybe our marriage wasn't officially over yet, but I knew that it was ending. Betraying our confidence, Josh called my dad and told him everything. When I got back to my parent's house, my dad gave me the cold shoulder and said that we needed to talk. I knew that he liked Josh. He said I was making a huge mistake. We planned to talk the next day on a walk around the park with the dogs.

That walk reminded me of the things I didn't like about my dad. I went with the intention of being honest, telling him that I was unhappy, and that I wanted a divorce. After counseling, I thought my dad and I were in a better place and I hoped that he would want me to make life decisions that led to happiness. I started telling him the truth, but he interrupted me in mid-sentence and said that leaving Josh would be the biggest mistake I could make. He emphasized that Josh was my financial freedom for the rest of my life, and that true love didn't matter. Just look at him and my mother.

I should have turned and walked away, but I poured my heart out hoping that maybe seeing his daughter so unhappy would bring him to support me. But he said if I left Josh, I wasn't welcome to live at his house anymore. In that moment, I clicked my dad goodbye for the second time. I was astounded that he thought so little of me that he thought I required someone else to provide my financial security. He couldn't understand that settling for comfort didn't work for me. Love was all that I wanted. For him, financial security was more important than love. Worse yet, I thought that his treatment of me revealed what he thought of my mother. We don't need happiness - we just need to cook, clean, have babies, and be grateful that we are supported.

Despite another falling out with my father, I was grateful that he and Josh had helped me start up my own business. I remembered that day. My family had gathered at one of my brother Kyle's soccer games. Josh had other plans and couldn't be there. Sitting at the game I talked about my current job at Fed Ex and said that while it was a wonderful job while I was in school, it was mindless, and I couldn't see myself loading and unloading boxes for the rest of my life. There had to be something more. My dad told me about a woman who deodorized used cars for car dealerships. He said there was little competition in the field and that the demand for the service was huge. He said that with my outgoing personality and being a hard worker, I would be a great candidate for that work.

My father sometimes surprised me with nice comments. We didn't always fight and sometimes it was pleasant to talk with him. I obviously wasn't getting a master's degree in business so that I could deodorize cars, but I was intrigued. He said the schedule was flexible, and as your own boss, income was dependent solely on your dedication to the work. I felt that this was something that I needed to consider. When I arrived home that night, I told Josh about the conversation with my dad. He thought it was a great opportunity and agreed to help with the upfront costs to start the business. I formed what I called Alpine Air Deodorization. That business became one of the best things that I've ever done, since it gave me security. While I don't think my father ever expected the success I have had, I'm grateful to him and Josh for helping.

I told my mom what had happened, and she said that she would stand by me no matter what. I was relieved that at least I had her support. I was still upset that when I told her that I wanted to call off the wedding, she talked me out of it. I guess that after years of being captive, she had come to view there were necessary trade-offs for financial security. I think my mom saw the clearer picture and just wanted me to be happy. After the falling out with my dad, I needed to find a place to live. I wasn't working, but I did have an independent contractor operating my business. I knew that I could make this work. I would find a place to live, get divorced, and finally start living on my terms.

I lived in my car for about a month. It was scary, but it was also thrilling. I could go anywhere and be anyone I wanted to be. I didn't have to go home to Josh or my Dad. I didn't have a home at all anymore. That was the scary part. Ironically, it gave me a sense of freedom, which was what I needed. I moved from trailhead to trailhead and climbed many peaks. When I needed a shower, I went to the 24-Hour Fitness gym where I was a member. I was homeless and living in my car. At the time it seemed great, but I knew it was temporary and that reality was around the corner.

Once, after grocery shopping at King Soopers, I was loading my car in the parking lot. The car bulged with stuff, and definitely looked "lived in." An older gentleman approached and gave me his card. He said a church that he worked for could help me find a place to live and that I didn't need to live in my car. I was shocked at first. If only this nice man knew my story but I didn't have all night to explain it, so I thanked him and said I was fine. I told him this was my choice and that, for now, I was happy. Driving away from King Soopers I felt shocked. *Did that man really think I was homeless? Am I homeless?*

Kevin introduced me to more of his friends that summer. After living out of my car for a few weeks, I reached out to my new friends, Matt and Brian, and told them what was going on. They offered me a room to rent in their house and I accepted. I was relieved to have a roof over my head again. I had signed up for my new unknown life. Now I had to live it, but at least I could live it on my terms.

John and I texted every day, and this kept me alive while craziness swirled around me. John had ignited new feelings in me. A week after we met, John invited me to come over to get some "one-on-one GPS training." I knew that it was really just an excuse to see me. John, in the midst of his divorce, had moved into a new condo. I arrived to find it empty except for a bed, a few pieces of furniture, his computer, and two chairs. He had taken little from his other home. He wanted nothing to remind him of his soon-to-be ex-wife. It was his new beginning.

I questioned my feelings for John, wondering if they were caused by my own divorce or if I was on a rebound. I always had male friends like Kevin and enjoyed hanging with them, but I'd never wanted an intimate relationship with them. John was different. I was attracted to this man, I had no idea why, and I didn't fight my feelings. It wasn't just that he was a climber because all of my friends were climbers and it wasn't just a physical attraction. There was something in his eyes and being that stirred my soul.

My GPS training with John that evening was exciting even though we sat in front of a computer. John showed me features on the GPS units and how to use tools on his website to display maps and markers on the units. I felt an intense chemistry with long gazes between our eyes. I behaved myself, but my feelings for John were real. I wasn't certain if he felt the same way about me, since he was getting divorced after a ten-year relationship and was devastated how things ended up.

I wondered if John was ready so soon to jump into another relationship, and I wondered at the same time, would I be ready? New feelings swirled in my head. *Was I pretty, smart, athletic, thin, and interesting enough to capture John's heart? Should I try to be coy, charming, sexy, or try to be anything?* I had to stop thinking that way. I was Alyson, a person falling in love with life and wanting someone like me to share it with. Life was complicated too, since I was still married. Josh and I had decided to end the marriage, but the process was just beginning. I yearned for a soul-mate, but I never expected him to appear so quickly.

We planned to meet the next Saturday night and climb peaks on Sunday. I fluttered with excitement all week waiting for our trip. It was two people getting together, and climbing peaks.

At first, I didn't tell anyone about John. My feelings were too new and fresh, and I wanted to protect them. I didn't want to taint them with my divorce. I didn't want to tell Kevin because I thought it would hurt his feelings. Kevin and I were friends, but I thought it was possible that stronger feelings were developing. Kevin helped me get up and get outside; he did so much for me I didn't want to hurt him.

I told my siblings about the divorce and, predictably, my brother Daniel was pissed off. He said I was messed up and that climbing ruined my marriage. He delivered a speech about ups and downs in marriage and how to stick together through the bad times. You try to do those things but it's not always so simple. You can hang in there and compromise and save the marriage, but there are limits. I had reached mine, and I tried to explain my position. Josh and Daniel were good friends, and I knew that it would take time for Daniel to get over this. I wished he knew that I'd tried to call off the wedding.

My sister Sarah and brother Kyle were also shocked. They weren't as close to Josh as Daniel, so they accepted my reasons and choices. Sarah supported me and wanted to see me happy. It wasn't just me divorcing Josh in a vacuum; my decision affected many people's lives. I knew that divorce was the right thing to do and I needed support, not speeches.

After a week of anticipation, I met John at the trailhead. I had driven to Vail Pass, parked and walked over to his car. I sat in the passenger seat beside him and we talked for hours. John was remarkable. I could look deeply into his eyes and see his soul. We shared pictures and stories, talked and laughed, and the rest of the world disappeared. We connected on a level I didn't know existed.

On Monday morning we climbed Uneva Peak and "Sneva Peak," which let us continue our conversation. We got to know each other better, and the more I learned about John, the more I thought we fit together. The looming question I asked myself was: *If John was the love of my life, how and when would I know?* We were two people where we wanted to be, doing what we wanted to do. Life could interfere and, of course, there were questions, but could this be it?

On Copper Mountain, our last peak, we decided to take a ski lift, which was free with a $20 purchase at the gift shop. With four Red Bulls in hand, we squished onto the lift seat. Our chemistry also soared and, not even considering a first kiss, I yearned for John to hold my hand. We made future plans for exciting adventures. I don't think John had ever met someone like me, a woman who shared his love of adventure. John was being careful, but I felt that he was falling for me as I was for him.

I still rented a room in Matt and Brian's house in the summer. I was usually away on trips, camping, and sleeping in my car, but I couldn't make future plans. My life was up in the air.

John and I made ambitious plans to climb in the San Juan Mountains for the weekend after the Uneva Peak hike. He took Friday off so we could leave Thursday night and spend three days together. I thought something should happen on this trip that would reveal John's thoughts. We hadn't yet had our first disagreement about anything.

My heart felt that this was my dream coming true. It seemed that all the pain and torment of the past few years and my recent accident had brought me to a new place. John's life and my crazy past life were eerily similar. Now, we were clicking our missing puzzle pieces into place. I could hear a counselor saying that I shouldn't be thinking about jumping into another relationship while I'm still married.

John and I enjoyed living on the edge. I loved mountains because they gave me an opportunity to massage my extreme personality, and John felt the same way. We had been stifled and confined in our respective marriages long enough. And now we were free to be who whoever we wanted. I thought that John and I were perfect for each other. I hoped he felt the same way.

I knew that my family and friends would disapprove of my new relationship. I also knew with a conviction born on Rosalie that I was doing the right thing for me. I was committed to thinking for myself. I chose not to be ruled by other's choices, actions, and reactions. Some people might sympathize, empathize, or support me but they didn't understand me. I felt that John was the first person who understood the real me. I decided to listen to my heart, not my head. As my eating disorder voice faded, I began cutting through the knots that held me captive.

# Chapter 19 – New Beginnings

The Leadville 100 race was scheduled for Saturday, August 20. In early August, Lynda asked about my recovery, and if I still wanted to pace her in the Leadville 100. I said yes. I told her that I had just run the Grand Mesa 50 and was climbing Thirteeners.

It was hard to believe that six months earlier, I'd been lying on the side of a mountain with a broken femur, not knowing if I would live or die. Lynda had appeared out of the darkness in a blizzard to rescue me. On the mountain, we'd talked about me pacing her in the Leadville 100 and I didn't forget that conversation. She believed in me. I had to believe in myself. My earlier life was riddled with a lack of confidence, but I was becoming more confident in myself so I could be the woman I was meant to be.

There were times during my recovery when I didn't believe that Leadville would happen, but Lynda encouraged me. I would pace her from the halfway point where racers turn around and run back on the same course. The course route goes over 12,540-foot Hope Pass and traverses grueling mountain terrain. After the Grand Mesa 50, I felt up for the challenge. Secretly, I hoped that pacing Lynda would help me run my own Leadville 100 one day.

## Race Across the Sky

We met at the Winfield aid station, the turnaround point of the race, at the ghost town of Winfield along Clear Creek. She looked strong, and we were off running. I felt fresh, and Lynda was resolute. We chatted as we climbed over Hope Pass flanked by Thirteeners that I had climbed in late July. When the sky darkened on the north side of the pass, we stopped to turn our headlamps on and have a quick drink.

Running in the darkness, I understood what a 100-mile race was like. We encouraged each other. We were two women tied together by an accident, doing what we loved, and proving that we could do it. Little by little I was learning to believe in myself and to accept that I was a capable person. I was running the Leadville 100 and pacing the woman who had saved my life. Lynda finished in 29:04:52, well under the cutoff time of 30 hours. I did what I promised on that dark night on Rosalie when Lynda told me that I was a survivor.

But now I wanted my own finish line. I remembered that Chris always wanted to run the Leadville 100, so I decided that one day I would run this legendary Race across the Sky as a memorial to him.


# San Juan Confessions

The San Juan Mountains, covering most of southwestern Colorado, is an amazing and beautiful region of towering mountain peaks. Most of the Colorado's mountain ranges are linear, and when you are there on the peaks, you look down onto populated valleys. By contrast, the San Juans cover a large circular area so it's easy to disappear deep into the mountains. Thirteen of Colorado's Fourteeners, along with hundreds of other peaks, scatter around the San Juans in sub-ranges like the San Miguel Range, Needle Mountains, and La Plata Range.

I fell in love with the rugged San Juans years earlier when I climbed the Fourteeners with Josh. The range is a long drive from Denver, often taking nine hours to reach the remote trailheads. The long drive insulates the peaks from casual weekend hikers that pour out of the Denver metro area. The San Juans were exactly where I wanted to go with John on our first weekend together.

A few days after the Leadville race, I met John at his condo and we loaded his Tacoma truck for the trip. I wasn't sure about the sleeping arrangements. I had a tent with me, but was used to sleeping in the back of my car. John also packed a tent, but thoughts of the alternatives made me nervous and excited.

I was also nervous about the two Thirteeners and a Twelver that we planned to climb. One was Coxcomb Peak, a hard mountain that requires roped pitches and a rappel to get across a notch on the summit ridge. I was determined to keep up with John to impress him. The other two peaks were easier but would take extra time.

After a long drive, we arrived at a trailhead along the West Fork of the Cimarron River near midnight. I asked John if we should set up both tents. Setting up two tents for a few hours of sleep didn't make sense, so we slept on the bed of the truck. I snuggled in my sleeping bag, butterflies in my stomach. I felt like a fifth-grade kid with a crush on a boy. We gazed at the starlit sky above. Without light pollution, the stars were impossible to process. I tried to identify the constellations and made a wish on a falling star. We lay there pretending to sleep, but I couldn't doze off with John lying next to me. I knew he was awake too. We lay for hours staring at the sky covering us like a soft blanket, trying to make sense of our feelings.

We must have slept, because we awoke to the alarm going off in the cold darkness. We put on our headlamps and cleaned up camp. We loaded our packs with a heavy rope and rock-climbing gear. I was tense because I had no idea what I was getting into. Coxcomb peak was going to be the hardest peak I had ever climbed. I was up for the challenge because I wanted to impress John. I had to try; I couldn't fail.

13,656-foot Coxcomb Peak made me both nervous and excited

We set off hiking, following a trail through flower-covered meadows surrounded by tall volcanic cliffs. We crossed a high pass above treeline, then climbed to the base of cliffs on Coxcomb. While hiking, I was lost in thoughts of John, and took sidelong glances at him. After seeing the first technical pitch up a steep chimney, I felt a surge of "can-I-do-this" anxiety.

We put on climbing harnesses, and John uncoiled the rope, set an anchor, and tied me into the rope's end. He stepped into the chimney, a wide fissure in the cliff, while I protected him from below by feeding the rope through a belay device clipped to my harness. I watched him gracefully move up the chimney. At the top of the pitch, he placed a belay anchor, pulled up the slack rope until it was tight against my harness, and called for me to start climbing. I wasn't an experienced rock climber and was out of my comfort zone. I put fear and doubt out of my mind and visualized standing on the summit with John. Then I went for it.

I started climbing the chimney, but when I reached the difficult moves, my weak left leg started shaking. My fear only made the shaking worse. This was my first experience with the infamous "Elvis" leg shake. John encouraged me with reassuring tugs on the rope. I felt connected to him, and completed the pitch by focusing on him and not my shaking leg. When I reached the belay ledge, I plopped down next to him on a ledge. I really needed a reassuring hug, but we were both apprehensive about getting too close. The hug would have to wait.

Alyson overcoming her Elvis leg shake on Coxcomb
Photo by John Kirk

We climbed onto Coxcomb's jagged namesake ridge where the view opened to the north. With my leg under control, we scrambled east along the ridge toward its highest point. When the summit seemed tantalizingly close, we reached a sharp notch that John had warned me about. I watched him set up a rappel line into the notch, and he told me what to do. I slid down the rope, letting the strands run through my device for a controlled descent. The climb up the other side of the notch was easier than I feared. At the top, we stood on Coxcomb's 13,656-foot summit. I felt happy and strong and knew I could do anything I set my mind to. But for now, I longed for a celebratory hug.

I was delighted to have climbed Coxcomb, one of Colorado's harder Thirteeners, just six months after my accident. This was the longest technical climb that I had ever done, and I had done it with John. If this was our first "date" then I wasn't falling in love, I was climbing into love. I couldn't contain my joy or pretend that I wasn't crazy about my new climbing partner.

We reversed the route, and headed over to 13,642-foot Redcliff to the north. We hurried since thunderstorms were building overhead. When we were halfway up Redcliff, the clouds unleashed hail, lightning, and booming thunder. We hunkered down to let the storm pass before heading to the summit.

It didn't matter if we sprinted, climbed technical pitches, rappelled, stood on summits, or hunkered down in a storm. We were infatuated with each another; oblivious to everything else in the world. I was climbing head over heels in love with this man. I pushed my old self-doubts away - even if John didn't think I was smart enough, pretty enough, thin enough, or athletic enough, I couldn't stop where my heart was going.

The storm passed, and we climbed to Redcliff's summit where we caught a whiff of ozone from the lightning. It was good that we had waited out the storm. I didn't want to be hit by lightning. The hair on my arms stood up, but it wasn't from an impending lightning strike. It was from knowing I was on the right life path.

I wanted to learn more about climbing safety, but John also interested me. When we reached a saddle below "U 4," our next peak, I asked, "John, what kind of person are you looking for in your next relationship?"

His immediate response was, "Someone exactly like you."

My leg felt weak again, and I just about fell over. My heart pounded, and my emotions twirled toward the sky. With embarrassed red cheeks, I balanced on my good leg, not knowing how to respond. It was the answer I wanted, but I was flustered. He must have known how taken I was with him. Even if I said nothing, my eyes betrayed me.

John asked, "What kind of person are you looking for in your next relationship?"

I said, "I think it's you!"

With smiles and peaks surrounding us, we savored that moment. We were happy. We were at the top of a mountain and high on a life we thought was only possible in dreams. Our San Juan confessions were simple, we were falling for each other, and there was the possibility of a long-term relationship. Standing on both of my legs, I couldn't have been in a better place.

A dramatic end on view of Coxcomb
Photo by Gerry Roach

We quickly hiked up "U 4," and when we got back to the car, I was filled with a sense of achievement. We had a successful and adventurous first hike together in the San Juan Mountains. We changed clothes and retreated to the old mining town of Ouray for dinner. We ate at Buen Tiempo on Main Street, and then crossed the street to Mouse's Chocolates for their famous scrap cookies. We logged onto John's website and entered our peaks for the day.

Shortly afterwards, Kevin texted me about climbing Coxcomb Peak. He asked who climbed it with me, and said that it was too soon after the accident for me to climb a difficult peak like Coxcomb. I told him that I was with John. I didn't want to tell Kevin because I didn't want to hurt him. He had done so much for me during my recovery. After not telling Josh the truth about our marriage, I wasn't going to get into the same predicament with Kevin. I explained that John and I were spending time together but avoided giving details.

When I was with John, I thought only of him. He elevated my body, spirit, and soul, and my problems disappeared. I had never felt happier or more alive. My emotions told me that John was my soul-mate, but my brain wondered what was going on. I was still married, and John was in the same situation. I wondered if we were moving too fast.

When we reached our next trailhead on Molas Pass, there was only one thing to do. We set up a tent and crawled inside. Surrounded by silence, we talked about the day and what tomorrow would bring. When silence found us, John reached over and took my hand. My butterflies flapped out of control. John held my hand outside the sleeping bags. I never knew these feelings existed. My heart raced, and I could barely breathe.

I'd found a new self, and needed to stick with it. I was getting a second chance at life, and nothing was going to stop me. I didn't know what struggles still loomed ahead, but for now, I just wanted to savor the adventures that John and I shared and marvel at my newfound feelings. The world was a different place as I drifted off to sleep next to a man I was falling in love with. I looked forward to tomorrow.

# Chapter 20 – My Future Finds Me

Josh and I moved ahead with our decision to divorce. We mostly texted, which wasn't the best way to communicate. A complication was my name on the loan for the Fruita home. Josh asked if we could put off the final divorce for six months so that he could refinance the loan and take my name off without incurring many penalties. I said absolutely, that wouldn't be a problem. We had ended the marriage, but would remain legally married for the next six months. We were free to move on and do whatever we wanted. It was hard to get divorced, but I knew we wouldn't have struggled as much if I had been honest from the beginning.

## Vestal Peak

John wanted me to do a backpacking trip with him on Labor Day weekend in September. He planned the trip and thought that it would be the best time for climbing. I had been backpacking once before, but nothing like what John had in store. He was going to show me the real thing.

I was nervous, since John had several difficult Thirteeners planned for the first day including 13,803-foot Arrow Peak, 13,864-foot Vestal Peak, and three other mountains called the Trinities. On day two we would climb Garfield, Graystone, and Electric Peaks and then hike out. These remote peaks form the heart of the Grenadier Range. They require a hefty effort to reach, with tricky routes over exposed terrain. This trip would surpass any day trip I had ever done.

Whenever John presented me with challenges, I jumped at the opportunity to join his fantastic adventures. Joining us on the trip was my friend Nick, whom I'd met before my accident and a mutual friend, Doug.

John and I had confessed our feelings for each other on the previous weekend. It was hard to tell if we were a couple yet, since everything was new. We had both been in marriages for the past decade, and I don't think either of us knew how to proceed in a new relationship.

Most Thirteeners offer more challenges compared to the popular Fourteeners routes. Most Thirteeners don't have trails, so they require good old-fashioned route finding and, assuming we stayed on route, the peaks also involved significant climbing. Vestal and Arrow were intimidating peaks that loomed above us during our hike to the campsite. I was nervous but knew that it would be a memorable adventure. Life has many dangers, but I knew I would have to take risks to achieve my goals. I could choose to sit at home, never venturing outside for fear of something bad happening and then slip in the bathtub and die. Risks are a part of life. I knew that climbing mountains put us at risk for injury or death, but I couldn't imagine a life lived otherwise.

Colorado's iconic Vestal and Arrow Peaks
Photo by John Kirk

We woke early on the first day and started toward Arrow Peak. John and I hiked fast and pulled ahead of Nick and Doug. We decided to race ahead and wait for them on the summit. This was not the recommended protocol, but we craved alone time. On the summit, John and I lapsed into a kiss fest. We had shared a first kiss the weekend before, and now we couldn't get enough kisses.

Nick and Doug eventually arrived and, after a brief celebration, we set off to Vestal. We stayed with Nick and Doug on the complicated traverse to Vestal, but still pushed the pace. When we arrived on Vestal's summit, Nick and Doug were exhausted, but John and I were just getting warmed up. Under darkening skies, we still needed to climb the Trinity peaks. The Trinity Traverse from Vestal across the three Trinity peaks requires careful route finding on loose rock and has some semi-technical sections. I knew that if I didn't climb them now, it could be a long time before I had another chance.

We descended Vestal, and then Nick and Doug headed for camp while John and I turned toward the Trinities. We waited out a thunderstorm, summited West Trinity, did a scary traverse, climbed a steep chimney, and reached the top of Trinity Peak, the highest of the trio. We continued traversing and finished up steep rock to the summit of East Trinity. We descended to a saddle below East Trinity and dropped down a steep gully toward a high lake above our campsite. We were tired after a long day of moving in the mountains. The sun dipped toward the horizon and its warm glow embraced us. I will always cherish the next moment. John arrived at the lake, looked back at me and smiled. I gave him my genuine Alyson smile. John said, "Your smile melts my heart."

His words were cheesy but also touching. At that moment, I knew that after almost dying on Rosalie, going through a divorce, and reconciling all my other heartaches that moment was worth it. I couldn't fully live life without a soul-mate. Finding a soul-mate is tough work, but if you spend the rest of your life with that person, it's life's greatest gift.

## Ice Lake Basin

Ice Lake Basin is an alpine cirque ringed with rugged mountains, including Vermilion Peak, Golden Horn, Pilot Knob, and Ulysses S. Grant Peak in the San Mountains west of Silverton.

These towering peaks dominate this special place, so it was an obvious choice to make a loop hike over its mountains. I had previously climbed Vermilion Peak, and was entranced by this magical basin filled with waterfalls, tundra meadows, and impressive peaks.

In early September we hiked into upper Ice Lake Basin and started the loop on 13,780-foot Golden Horn. Its spectacular summit was unforgettable. We scrambled to the top and sat amid scenic splendor. John took my hand and said that he loved me. I told John that I loved him too. I had waited so long to tell him, even though we had only known each other a few months. We sat and looked into each other's eyes, and time seemed to stand still.

13,780-foot Golden Horn, our first "I Love You" summit
Photo by John Kirk

The next peak was Pilot Knob, which gave one of my scariest experiences yet. We climbed up exposed loose shelves of rock, and then traversed a sloping slab littered with decomposing rock below a cliff above a fatal drop-off. John said not to think about the drop-off and to focus on the next move. My new life goal was simple:

197

don't fall. I tried hard to put my fears aside and trust in John, but halfway across both of my legs began shaking. John calmly gave me instructions. I only needed to breathe and trust in my abilities. Beyond the traverse, we scrambled to the top where I screamed, "Yes!" The thrill outweighed my fear, and on my way back across the traverse, I wondered what the fuss was about.

Alyson scampering to 13,738-foot Pilot Knob's summit
Photo by John Kirk

Next, we hiked toward "V 4," another ranked Thirteener in the San Juans. The climbing route offered pinnacles, cliffs, and steep slopes glazed with loose stones that skated beneath my feet like marbles. When I was afraid, I paused to gaze at the stupendous surroundings and John scampering ahead. Three deep breaths and everything was okay again. Focusing on the next move, I found John on the rocky top and we embraced on our third summit of the day.

Relaxing on top of the peak, I glanced at my watch and then at the challenging terrain ahead. I didn't know if I had another peak in me. I decided this is what I'm living for—excitement, adventure, and sharing it with John. Of course, I could do another peak.

John pointed at our final mountain, Ulysses S. Grant Peak, and said, "No one has reported combining all of these peaks before." I stared at U. S. Grant. It looked magnificent and difficult. The peak commanded its own cirque with a small island in the middle of a circular lake. I looked at the map and saw that the tarn was named Island Lake. The picturesque scene looked like a postcard.

U. S. Grant Peak was spectacular as we traversed toward it. Above a saddle, we followed a faint trail. Higher, we moved carefully up exposed rock and then into a steep gully which led to the summit. I hugged John in the late afternoon glow and breathed in his ear, "I love you." U. S. Grant Peak became one of our favorite peaks. We stared in every direction from the summit, gobbling up the expansive views, but our eyes kept returning to the island in the lake below. It seemed like a fantasy, so serene, isolated, and beautiful.

13,767-foot Ulysses S. Grant from "V 4"
Photo by John Kirk

Alyson nearing the summit of U. S. Grant Peak
Photo by John Kirk

Island Lake seen descending from U. S. Grant Peak
Photo by John Kirk

In the middle of September, John landed a new job that he would start in early October. I was still on leave from FedEx, and had someone running my company, so we were both free. I could return to Fed Ex anytime, but decided to take advantage of the leave of absence for six months. I was reinventing myself and thrilled to play in the mountains with John as long as I could. Nothing else was important to me at that moment. I knew things would change, but for once in my life I was living in the moment and loving it.

Our next weekend adventure was John's plan to complete the five-peak traverse near Conundrum Hot Springs. John spoke of this loop on the first day I met him and here we were doing the loop a few months later. After a long day with many dicey sections and a long hike out, we were successful - another combination that no one had reported completing. We drove to a campsite at the Lost Man Trailhead for the next day's climb.

Early the next morning, we launched across a ridge traverse over five ranked peaks called the Williams Group near Independence Pass in central Colorado's Sawatch Range. Rugged Williams Mountain is the highest peak in the group.

Despite my best efforts to keep up, John pulled ahead near the top of an easy peak, an unnamed 13,033-foot mountain, the first peak on the traverse. When I reached the rounded summit, John was talking to his mom on the phone. After hanging up, John said that she really wanted to meet me, and that he wanted me travel to El Paso, Texas for Thanksgiving to meet his family.

Talk about moving fast. I had just met John in August, and now I'm going to meet his parents. I asked myself what I was getting into, but I knew the answer. It was the speed of the relationship that gave me pause.

I plopped down next to John and he told me about his parents. He said they were unique, and that I had nothing to worry about. He said I had to go and he wouldn't take no for an answer. I looked at my options, which were go with John or stay in Colorado by myself. Most of my family wasn't talking to me, so the first option sounded best. Perhaps John's family would like me. If they didn't I would be trapped in a place with people I didn't know. I decided they would like me since I'm a good person who loves their son and he loves me. I kissed John and said yes.

# Our Fireside

On September 28, John and I drove toward the San Juan Mountains. On the way, we stopped at Crested Butte to enjoy the golden aspen colors and climb a group of five peaks, topped by 12,958-foot Purple Mountain. Aside from the Thirteeners, I learned that John planned to climb Colorado's 1,000 highest peaks, roughly everything higher than 12,500 feet. We found a perfect campsite on the West Fork of the Cimarron River in the northern San Juans.

We strode up valley on a crisp morning, then cut up toward "Fortress Peak." The route up Fortress required clever route finding through complex cliffs and crumbling pinnacles composed of volcanic tuff. Eroded from an old volcano, this peak offered an airy summit and otherworldly views. Sitting on the summit, we gazed at Coxcomb where my leg had learned the Elvis Shake. Moving down valley, we found a similar route up Precipice Peak. The peak, visible from the highway, has a sheer 700-foot-high north face. We snuck up through pinnacles of weathered rock to its summit.

Since my accident, I loved fires and their smell. The scent of the rescuers' fire was etched in my memory. That smell meant life. We decided to make a fire that evening. We pitched our tent, and I brought a blanket over to the fireside. John and I sat and gazed into each other's eyes beside the warm fire. He stared so deeply into my eyes that I swore he could read my mind.

Our itinerary for the next day was more ambitious. We planned a long traverse over a committing group of five mountains called the Twilight Range. This small San Juan sub-range nestles between the Grenadiers to the east and the western San Juan Mountains.

We topped out on North Twilight Peak first, then started a traverse. The descent to the saddle between North Twilight and Twilight was easy, but then the climbing became more difficult as we threaded through cliffs. Higher, we made short work of an easy traverse to South Twilight Peak. We had two peaks to go. The views were spectacular.

We dropped down a cliff and gully to reach Point 12,932, a ranked Twelver. Then, we climbed the steep north side of 13,062-foot West Needle Mountain. After traversing under South Twilight back to Crater Lake and the trail, we ran back to the trailhead. Flush with life and love, we paused on our drive home to dash up Flat Top, a small peak north of Montrose. The mountain didn't matter, only our stride, breath, and togetherness.

## Am I Crazy?

Since pacing Lynda in the Leadville 100, my desire to run a 100-mile race had increased. After training in September, I wanted to do something big before winter arrived. I knew that it seemed crazy to run 100 miles so soon after my accident, but I had already run two 50-mile races. I knew I would have pain in my leg and I might have to drop out, but I was good at enduring pain, so I figured I would try the longer race.

I browsed the race websites and found the Slickrock 100-mile run in Moab, Utah, which was scheduled for October 8. I immediately wanted to do it and, on sheer impulse, registered for the race. This was just the challenge that I sought. It was now my turn to throw an adventure at John, so I asked if he would pace me for the last 50 miles. He agreed, and the race was on. John wasn't a runner, but he said he would do this for me.

I told my sister, Sarah, about the race and she said I was crazy. I agreed, and she had no choice but to wish me luck. I decided to not tell the rest of the family since they wouldn't understand. John was with me and that was all the support I needed.

Despite positive visualizations, I was nervous about the race, since I had never run over 50 miles and didn't know what to expect. I remembered the awful leg pain I had in the Grand Mesa 50 and hoped it wouldn't come back. Since that race, I had packed in almost three months of intense training.

We camped with most of the runners near the starting line. The predawn start arrived before I could think about it and I was off. The first fifty miles were tougher than I expected, but I enjoyed the beauty of the sandstone landscape. After running for hours, I approached the 50-mile aid station where John waited for me.

Dashing into the station, I saw John and his smile energized me. I grabbed new supplies and water, and took off. After running

50 miles, most ultra-runners experience the feeling that it seems impossible to run another 50 miles. That thought wore off as we ran into the sunset.

As we ran through the quiet night, I became lost in thought and pondered the last year and what I was doing. Perhaps it was a runner's high, but I was proud of myself. As deeper memories surfaced, I remembered being an obese, drug-using alcoholic, who smoked a pack of cigarettes a day. I felt like shouting, "Look at me now!" I didn't need anyone else to be proud of me; my self-pride was sufficient. It was beyond time for blaming my dad for everything bad in my life. I was an adult ready to take my share of responsibility for who I had become.

Reality has a habit of poking through the most precious moments. By mile 80, someone had a hammer and was pounding on my leg. The pain was almost unbearable, but I convinced myself that pain is only temporary. I knew that finishing this run would be nothing short of a miracle.

By mile 90, we had slowed to a fast walking pace, and the leg pain had subsided. Only ten miles to go. Every step brought me closer to the finish line. My formula was simple: relentless forward motion. I began hallucinating at 2:30 in the morning. John could tell I was cold, so he grabbed my hand and squeezed tight. The warmth and pressure made all the difference. Walking under a bright moon and star-filled sky, the last miles of my first 100 passed.

Moments after crossing the finish line, I flung my arms around John, kissed him, and knew that this was one of my best experiences. I finished the Slickrock 100 in 22 hours and 16 minutes. Not too shabby for a 28-year-old woman who had broken her femur eight months earlier. Anything seemed possible. I was building self-confidence and redefining myself.

John started his new job after Slickrock, but continued to plan multi-peak hiking loops for the weekends, while I pursued my new life. I regularly heard John say, "These peaks have never been combined before." Our adventures convinced me that we could do anything together.

# Chapter 21 – Happy New Year

We made the 12-hour drive from Denver to El Paso over Thanksgiving weekend. Along the way, we scrambled up small peaks near the highway. I wondered if John's parents would wonder why it took us so long to get there, but John assured me that they understood his mountain climbing passion. I hoped he was right. I reminded myself that we were adults, free to make our own choices.

My nerves rattled as we approached El Paso. So much had happened to John and me during the past six months, and now I was meeting his folks. Not surprising given my family history, I thought, *I hope they like me, but what if they don't? I'm sure they want the best for their son, Am I the best? Do I have all the qualities that John's parents would hope for*?

Remembering my last in-laws chilled me, not because I didn't care about them, or because they weren't great people, but the prospect of having new in-laws so soon seemed absurd. Josh and I dated for almost five years before he proposed. Now, I thought, I'm still married and have dated John for three months. I told myself to calm down and not panic.

Trying to control my nerves, we walked to the front door and rang the bell. Seconds later, Bud and Peggy Kirk stood in the doorway with big grins. Bud was tall, wore glasses, had white hair and was cute for an older man. Peggy was shorter, had long hair, wore lots of jewelry, and offered a smile that warmed a stranger's heart. Peggy looked at us, grinned harder, and then hugged me. She said she was happy that I'd come. A huge sense of relief washed over me.

After meeting the Kirks, I felt like I had known them my entire life. They grabbed our bags, took them to the guest room, and made us feel at home. I had wondered if we should stay in separate bedrooms, and about how his parents felt about us sharing a room. It wasn't an issue. We stayed for a week on one of my most memorable trips. The Kirks were astonishing people, and I realized that I was fortunate to have them in my life.

Alyson, John, Peggy, and Bud

The Kirks were genuinely interested in what John and I did. They wanted to know about mountain ranges we visited and the peaks we climbed. My family had no interest in my activities, so this interest was foreign to me. It was a treat to have John's parents interested in our lives. Every day we left to climb local peaks and then returned to spend time with them in the evening. Bud and Peggy didn't judge me, they just accepted me.

Peggy and Bud had their own craziness, and that's why I think they related to us. They embraced their own passions and encouraged everyone else to do the same. Peggy is the world's best shopper, while Bud loves fishing and tinkering with things on their farm. Both still worked but took time out to enjoy what they loved. They also loved John and accepted him as his own person. They wanted us to be happy. I could see where John got his drive to never do anything half-way. It was whole hog or nothing with his parents.

Peggy told me about John's ex-wife. She said that the timing of our romance couldn't have been better. She was thrilled that John was happy for the first time in many years, and she attributed that to falling in love with me. She said she was worried about John and the dark place he had been trapped in.

It was sad leaving the Kirks and heading back to Denver. I had just met these people, but it felt like they had been part of my life for a long time. I loved them and hoped they would become part of my life.


## Moving Right Along

When John and I returned from El Paso, we decided to live together. I still had my stuff at a friend's house and didn't stay with John every night. We just couldn't have that anymore. We couldn't deny how we felt about each other, and we wanted to be together all the time. It was easy for me to decide.

When I told my mom I was moving in with John, she nearly had a heart attack. I was still married to Josh and our divorce wouldn't happen until March after he finalized the house refinance. John was now divorced, and I reasoned that my temporary legal status shouldn't stop me from moving. We told Peggy the news and she was happy for us, and that warmed my heart. She wanted her son to be happy and she saw that happiness when we were together. Having their support meant the world to both of us.

Bud and Peggy decided to visit us for Christmas. Since I was on the outs with my own family, I spent most of the holiday with John and his parents. We introduced John's parents to Jim, Cappy, and my mom. It was awkward at first, but things were fine once they discovered that we just wanted to be happy.

My life was moving in the right direction, although I sometimes had my old ED thoughts. In rational moments, I knew that there was something wrong with reverting to self-destructive behavior when things got rough. The ED voice had been my constant companion for so long that it seemed okay to listen to it now and then.

I had found John, my soul-mate. I thought at this point the old voice would disappear. I guess it's not that easy. Life is full of bumps and scrapes no matter which route we take. We are never completely free from turmoil. I knew that I had chosen this path and decided the bumpy ride was worth it. My new life wasn't perfect, but it was getting there. We were determined to overcome obstacles and to focus on the good things in our lives. I knew I could overcome my eating disorder voice and behavior once and for all by living authentically and having the support I always needed.

## Elephant Butte

After John's parents headed home after Christmas, John and I decided to spend New Year's weekend somewhere warm. The Moab area was dry and a good option. John mentioned that he wanted to take me up Elephant Butte, one of his favorite peaks. The butte, the highest point in Arches National Park, provided a climb through fins and canyons that I would never forget.

The Elephant Butte adventure includes scrambling, a couple rappels, and a few tricky spots. John said that on the descent we would do a free rappel down a cliff. I asked what a free rappel was. I had rappelled before but it scared me. John described Elephant Butte's free rappel. He said I would stem down a V-shaped sandstone slot to a set of bolt anchors. Then, I would thread the rope through my belay device and slide down the rope and over an edge. Below an overhang, my feet would leave the rock and I would swing into thin air, hanging only by the rope. John brushed my fears aside and told me to remember that it was safe, and that the rappel would add excitement to an already spicy day.

5,653-foot Elephant Butte in Arches National Park
Photo by John Kirk

We arrived in Moab on New Year's Eve. It was chilly and there was almost no snow on the ground. We hiked up some lower peaks on the last day of my memorable year.

We climbed Elephant Butte on New Year's Day, 2012. We headed up a rock-walled canyon, taking improbable turns and climbing slabs that I didn't think I could climb down. Near the top, we worked up a crack that broke through an upper cliff. Above the slope relented, and we zipped over to the summit. We found the register on the slickrock top and enjoyed 360-degree views across the colorful desert and a fairyland of fins, arches, causeways, and secret spots.

John acted differently that day, so I thought it was because he was taking me on a harder climb. Maybe he was distracted because of the free rappel. We signed the register, and John gave me a kiss. It was a wonderful way to start the New Year. Then John pulled out a small box, opening it to reveal a diamond sparkle, and said, "I think we need to get married."

Speechless and overwhelmed, I said, "What the...?" I looked at the stunning ring in the box John held, and said, "Yes, Yes, Yes!"

On top of Elephant Butte on January 1, 2012 - Just Engaged!
Selfie by Alyson Kirk

I didn't expect a proposal from John. I was married and engaged at the same time. That was one of the best moments in my life. The thought of being John's wife sent my soaring emotions into orbit. I felt like the happiest person alive. My past decisions had been the right ones and my choices had brought me to that moment.

We embraced, kissed, and soaked in the short January day. I wanted to stay up there forever, but knew that we still had an exciting free rappel ahead of us.

We climbed down toward the rappel station, stemming through the tight slot. At the anchors, John set up the rope and threaded it through my rappel device. It was time for me to go backward. Looking down, the abyss below didn't seem as deep as the one I had teetered over for most of my pre-accident life. I could do it.

Alyson, engaged for 10 minutes and heading for the abyss
Photo by John Kirk

When I reached the last step before dropping over the edge, my heart pounded. It was too much to handle all at once. With John's proposal, I swam in deep emotions and now, I had to drop into thin air. I had to trust John's expertise. I took a step and then swung down and hung free in the desert air.

I was petrified, but after a moment I focused on the rock wall that was only a few feet away, on my belay device, and the rope. I let the rope slip through my device. I wasn't falling, so I continued sliding down the rope. I was suspended in the center of a large sandstone amphitheater. It looked like a good echo chamber, so I let loose with a wild, "Yes!" Echoes of my voice spiraled across the desert.

# Chapter 22 – Fast Forward

Since pacing Lynda in the Leadville 100, we did several climbs together and built a unique friendship. On one of our hikes, I asked Lynda if she would climb Rosalie Peak with me on the one-year anniversary of my accident, weather permitting. She immediately accepted my invitation and we made plans to revisit the peak on February 19, 2012. My accident anniversary approached and I couldn't believe that a full year had passed since my life-changing struggle. The weather forecast wasn't good. In fact, it was similar to what it had been the year before. I told Lynda that this time I would be hiking out on my two feet.

## Resolution on Rosalie

Driving to the trailhead, long shadows sliced the naked trees, while high clouds cast a pall over the mountains. We silently prepared for the climb and started up the trail. Once we were in motion, the snow-packed route triggered flashbacks. As we hiked, I recounted the entire ordeal to Lynda. I remembered where the snowmobile had picked me up and where the fire roared. Looking at the snow-covered fire circle, I did a double-take, imagining that I could smell the fire. We continued hiking to treeline and decided to summit Rosalie first, and then visit the accident site on the descent.

A sharp wind greeted us on Rosalie's summit. As I took in the 360-degree view of snowcapped mountains, I felt a weight lifted from me. I needed to stand atop Rosalie and thank the mountain for its gift, a second chance at life.

After a short stay, the wind urged us to leave. Heading down, we used the GPS coordinates from the previous hike to navigate to the accident site. As we approached the spot from above, I recoiled from the memory of the fall. With weakened bones, one step had nearly killed me. I could sense the shock of my fall, the snap of my bone, and the agony on the ice-cold slab of granite. I tried hard to keep from crying and get my nerves under control. I reminded myself that this visit was something I needed to do.

Standing at the same spot with two strong legs, I was a pile of mixed emotions. Flashbacks and memories twisted through my mind. I calmly untwisted them one by one, soaked them with a year's time, and made my peace. I remembered my deal with God. I looked at Lynda and saw the same caring face that had saved me the year before. I thought of Prakash and the kind people who had done their best to get me off this mountain alive. I owed them so much.

I placed an imaginary bundle of feelings of anger, hate, and resentment on the slab that I had carried with me for most of my life. I told myself that I was free of the burdens holding me down. The things that had hurt me the year before were gone, and I was a different person. I asked the wind to blow the pieces of my bundled burdens into oblivion so that I could never find them again, and then I could move forward.

I had stuck by my promises. The path had not been easy, but I'd used my second chance to turn my life around. I was happy. I felt that Chris was there with me, thanking the mountain that changed me. I was awash with a feeling of achievement and relief. I survived and now I'm living authentically. I made a second promise to stick with my plan. Tears ran down my cheeks as the memories of my ordeal rushed through my mind. I silently thanked the mountain for the gift of a new life. I couldn't speak.

The air was brighter when we reached the trailhead and now matched my mood. I made my peace with the mountain with the woman who had helped save me. I thanked Rosalie for my new opportunity. I was at peace. I was happy. I had found John. I had found myself.


## Doubters

As our relationship progressed, John and I developed a reputation within Colorado's peakbagging community. People were compelled to say disdainful things about us. We heard bits and pieces of the gossip, but also knew that the doubters didn't know our situation. We heard that the relationship was doomed - that we were a train wreck waiting to happen. Some gave us six months maximum. I'm sure that worse things were said, but remained hidden.

On John's website, you can see which peaks the members are climbing, so people saw the long loop hikes that John and I had done over the past months. We usually hiked more peaks than most of the members. We had also both gone through life-changing experiences with my accident and both of us getting divorced. I wasn't working and John was between jobs. Our lives were at a turning point, and while not working I had a lot of time to be free. I knew this wasn't going to last forever, but I thought while I wasn't working and reinventing myself, I should enjoy the free time to my fullest and that is exactly what I did. "Real life" would be back before I knew it.

Honestly, many climbers couldn't do what we were doing. The mountains offer the same challenge to everyone. We heard that we were doing it for the wrong reasons, but we didn't understand what the wrong reasons were. We were driven by our love of mountains and there is nothing wrong with that. We were told that we were obviously not enjoying our climbs. That was laughable. These were the most joy-filled days of my life. I ran through fields of fragrant flowers and I often smelled more flowers in a week than some people do in a lifetime. We savored every minute of our ascents. John and I loved hiking the big loops and were young and fit enough to do them. I had gone big with my running, even doing 100-mile races. Going big was natural for John and me.

Even Kevin sent me an email with a quote from one of his friends stating that, "The more peaks you climb, the bigger loser you are." Kevin knew my passion for peaks, had encouraged me to start hiking again, and to chase my goals like climbing all the Thirteeners. Things became difficult when I fell in love with John. I was grateful to Kevin for helping me after my accident to get outside again and do what I loved. I was scared and Kevin was important in my recovery, and I thank him for caring.

No matter what you do, there will always be people who criticize you. I find it's best to ignore them. If we believe every negative thing said to us, we would spend our lives in a downward spiral while trying to please everyone else. John and I loved what we did, so what anyone else said didn't matter to us.

People didn't realize that I had spent decades on the other side of the fence, longing to be free. It took a long time to reach that point in my life. The addictions that hurt me, like alcohol, cigarettes, and drugs, were worth eliminating, and I would help someone solve those problems or get help. Overcoming an eating disorder is tougher and it took me years to realize that it's a life-long struggle.

Some people devote their lives to raising children, not considering that their own passions are also important. Children learn best by example and need to know that it's okay to follow their dreams. I have running friends with children who continue to race. One friend tried to get into the Hardrock 100 race for years. The race has a lottery, so it's difficult to be accepted. She had a two-year-old daughter and was pregnant with her son when she was accepted into Hardrock. She had three months to drop the baby weight, get in shape, and run the race. She did it. I'm not suggesting that our passions should take precedence over the needs of children, but there should be a balance.

# Chapter 23 – A Daring Adventure

As John opened up about his past, it was obvious why we were cathartic for each other. Unlike my trials, the details of John's marriage were hard to hear. During the first few months of our relationship, we spent a lot of time together hiking and driving. Some of the trips involved four- to six-hour drives. There was no better way to pass the time than to talk. On these road trips we opened up and let it all out. We learned just about everything about the other person.

I wanted to know the gory details of John's marriage, what went wrong, and when. On one drive to the San Juans, he let it all out. John described his life in detail when it started spiraling out of control with his marriage falling apart and his divorce.

"I awoke desperate to catch my breath. Where was I? Lying on a discarded bed in the basement, I hadn't gotten the rest I'd hoped for and could not shake a throbbing headache, a reminiscent of a hangover. This was now a recurring pattern.

"I'd had two-and-a-half hours of sleep, interrupted by a reliving of my wife's recent screaming and ranting about my unhealthy obsession with mountains. This had happened despite the conversation we'd had earlier in the week about my plans, when she displayed no sign of disapproval. I'd been prepared to sleep for six hours, but she would have none of it. I had been climbing mountains for a decade, and now, at her insistence, I was faced with the decision to say goodbye to my life's passion. Little did I know at the time, she had been engaging in an obsession of her own for quite some time when she left the house, which had become increasingly frequent."

As John described his marriage falling apart, I heard his words and could relate to what he said. It felt the same, but it was so different. I let John continue.

"The day didn't begin as an ambitious trip. I had a few 9,000-foot peaks in mind southwest of Cañon City, with a good bit of trail.

Unfortunately, I had plenty of time to contemplate the one-sided conversation that had taken place the night before—and the many times before. She had complained to my mother over the last year about how selfish I was to not give up hiking and climbing. Recently, even my family urged me to 'give up hiking' to save my marriage."

I interrupted John here because what he was saying was identical to what I went through. I pointed out we had both had our families and spouses urge us to give up our passions to please them. At the time, we both felt like continuing to climb mountains was the wrong thing to do. John continued.

"I wrestled back and forth with my thoughts, caught in a tug-of-war between guilt and anger. I began to think that maybe there was something wrong with me for prioritizing my happiness. At the same time, I wondered what the purpose of all this was. Are we simply meant to exist vicariously and breed like cattle with no self-fulfillment, ambition, or drive? Is an 'average life' really what I'm after? Is the body of human experience enriched or enhanced by those who shun or dispose of their passion or obsession? This is not to say there is something wrong with being 'normal' or a vicarious product of herd mentality. It's that I know I'm hardwired for something else.

"Everything was simpler in my early adulthood. I didn't struggle with these thoughts. I had the answer. I remember when I was 19, halfway into my ninth beer at 1:00 in the afternoon, drinking alone in a Jeep at the base of Ski Santa Fe, when I had an epiphany: 'This is it. This is what it's all for.' The 'it' was the alternate reality of intoxication. Throughout college and graduate school, I 'rewarded' myself after the weekday grind with drinking binges. I didn't need to think about my life's meaning or what I could really experience instead of simply existing. I wasn't concerned about the trappings of 'the script,' to mindlessly simulate the life pattern of their predecessors. Alcohol served me well to mask the lack of meaning in my life. It was the elixir for the unremarkable."

I felt John's words deeply. How could we have had so many past life similarities? God only knew how much I related to what John was saying about his struggles with alcohol. There had been so many times in my past that I thought getting drunk or high was what life was all about. That that was "as good as it gets."

John continued, "My soon-to-be ex-wife and I had the passion of drinking in common when we first met. We followed the steps everyone else expected, but I don't believe we ever really knew each other, ourselves, or what we were really about. So, I came to adhere to the pattern of marriage, career, and struggling to experience something more redeemable than my own life through TV. I drank daily, and true to my nature, I never did anything I liked half-heartedly."

John's words hit me to the core. Almost everything he said was something I had gone through or struggled with. We were the same people in different lives who wanted something more. As he spoke I got chills. How can we have had such similar past lives and met one another at the turning point in both our lives. I could only think it was fate that brought us together.

John relayed more from his past life. "Early on, I climbed mountains, and was especially obsessed with Colorado's Fourteeners. My habitual passion, however, was checking out of life with a twelve-pack, which seemed especially rewarding after a hard day in the mountains. Eventually, I had to reassess this passion. I didn't like not being in control of things I said when I was drinking. I knew that the amount I drank wasn't healthy. My job wasn't healthy either, adding more desire to 'numb out' at the end of the day. I was diagnosed with high blood pressure at 29. I attempted to cut back on my drinking, and thought if I could get a better job, maybe I'd quit.

"Late in 2005, things started to change. I pushed back at work and interviewed successfully for a new job. On my last working day of the year, my climbing friend Kurt picked me up and we met friends downtown for dinner. He was making an attempt at sobriety. After dinner we talked at length, parked in my driveway. I said I thought I would quit as a New Year's resolution, but I needed to stop at the liquor store since my new job didn't start until the day after New Year's Day. As we talked, I realized that if I was really going to quit then saying I'm going to quit later wasn't being true to myself.

"The next day, I snowshoed up Deer Mountain near Estes Park in a cathartic, bittersweet farewell to a dominant force in my life. I didn't know what the future held, but I knew it would be different. I never made it back to the liquor store."

More chills. I had dealt with a drinking problem like John. I often rewarded myself by having a drink or two or twelve. At one point I felt that drinking was my passion and something I would do for the rest of my life.

"I really thought that my marriage would improve. Although, after removing what had brought us together, I must have become much less interesting. My ex-wife would often say, 'You're no fun since you can't drink socially' or 'It's awkward to have you along at my friends' places because you don't drink or eat red meat. She also refused to work, insisting that she needed to stay in college, despite acquiring a bachelor's degree 11 years prior. I was paying for her to take seven more years of college. This wasn't really a marriage of teamwork.

"Over time, I began climbing more mountains, listing them, and pushing myself to higher physical standards. My ex-wife tried to convince me that my obsession with mountaineering was simply a manifestation of alcoholism.

"I made my way south to climb another four peaks, thinking that my days in the hills could be numbered. I called my spouse on the drive home and said that we needed to work things out and get help."

She said, "Why are you saying this now?"

"That wasn't the response I'd expected, and I struggled for words. I told her I was willing to do what she had asked - to quit climbing. Later in the week I talked to my mother on the phone. She said that my spouse called her and told her that she wanted out of the marriage and that I refused to work on it. Things were turning bizarre, and she was finding more reasons to not be at home. When she was home, she was engrossed in her phone.

"She wanted to go out Friday night and said I should go climb mountains on Sunday. After her night out, she didn't return until Saturday morning. I knew she'd go drinking 'with friends,' and it was annoying when she would show up at home after her promised time, but I trusted her. That is until she shared 'an idea.' After finishing my last peak on Sunday afternoon, I called to confirm when I'd be home. She told me to keep climbing if I wanted because she had an important idea that could repair our marriage. Huh? That didn't make sense, but I hustled home."

She said, "What do you think about an open marriage?"

Thinking that I must have misheard, I replied, "What exactly do you mean?"

"I need to experience being wanted sexually by people other than just you. Don't you think we'd both enjoy having more partners?"

"No, the thought makes me sick."

"I thought this was a joke or ploy, but I knew something wasn't right about all the mornings she'd come home and all the time she spent on the phone and Facebook. I finally got the nerve to ask what was going on after she didn't show up on a Wednesday night until 3:00 in the morning. I found out what had really been happening in my marriage for over a year."

I felt a mixed bag of emotions as I listened to John describe the situation. My end of my marriage was nothing like this. I don't know what I would have done if Josh told me that he wanted an open marriage. I would probably be disgusted and hurt. John was getting upset as he revisited this painful time. I hoped his explanation helped him let go of his past and some of the pain.

"I didn't have to look hard to discover lots of emails and Facebook messages that revealed her double life. She wasn't just having an affair, but multiple affairs with a procession of guys, some of whom I knew, including a group of contractors who worked on our house. I kept reading and discovered that it became worse."

"Her encounters were beyond anything that I ever imagined. She wasn't just wrecking our marriage, but other people's relationships as well. Impervious and oblivious, she just kept going. One message from a woman begged her to stop texting her husband about sodomy while they were having a family dinner.

"I felt an overwhelming shock and horror at her double life. I was used to being in control of my body, but my chest tightened and I breathed with short sharp gasps. I had to formulate a plan to leave immediately.

"We hear stories about people living in basements during divorces, but the stories seem foreign until you've been there. When it's your story, you instantly know things can never be the same again. My life with her had become a dark place. I called my parents and told them I was leaving my marriage. My mother begged me to try marriage counseling. I told her that I would email her some messages and she would know why I couldn't stay any longer. After my mother read the emails there was a long silence. Finally, she said to get out as quickly as possible. She feared for my safety. My parents were completely supportive of my decision.

"A friend at work was remodeling a house and offered to let me rent the basement, which was already finished. After leaving her, I had a damaged outlook on relationships and imagined that I'd spend the rest of my life alone. But at least now, I'd be free of the screaming and nagging. Nothing, however, could prepare me that these events weren't even close to the depths my soon to be ex-wife would descend to.

"As the weeks passed, I tried to focus on projects that would result in positive change, like job interviews and finding a new place to live. I wasn't focused on work, which was a drain with recent management changes, so I was motivated to find a new job. It seemed like closing this life chapter was going to be a long process. My rock bottom had nothing to do with alcohol or substance abuse. Apparently, life is torturous enough without those problems.

"I spent the first few evenings working on divorce forms and financial statements, trying to expedite the process, which takes 90 days minimum after filing. Strangely, I was having some of the best sleep of my life."

Wow! I thought when John finished telling me the story of his marriage. The end of my marriage was nothing like that so I really felt for John. We both had pain from broken marriages and wanted more for our lives. Next, John told me about how he and I first met and what that was like for him.

"I was in touch with Kevin, a peakbagger who had also recently been divorced. We talked about a group hike to climb some 13,000-foot peaks near Aspen. Kevin had been hiking up mountains with a woman known by the mysterious handle 'TripleM' on my website. I'll never forget that morning when I was greeted with 200 lumens shining directly in my eyes. That was the first time we met."

I remembered the morning like it was yesterday and remembered John saying, "Wow, that's a powerful headlamp you have there!"

Later that day John and I shared stories about our eminent divorces and failed attempts to change for others. I talked about my former life when I was overweight. The overweight reference made everyone laugh—John said I had the body of an athlete or model. No one could picture what I looked like, but I knew the truth and I had pictures to prove it.

We continued comparing past and present. It was eerie how similar John and my lives were. John and I had quit drinking after full-fledged alcoholism; we each endured years of criticism and attempts to derail our passion for mountains; we were both successful in business; we avoided red meat; and we wanted to climb every peak. John told me how lucky he was to be with an upbeat, energetic woman with a dark past who had just run a 50-mile race a few months after breaking her femur in a serious accident.

He said, "I didn't think anyone like you could actually exist. Your drive and perseverance are impressive."

John and I became each other's therapy, reaching for the heights and sharing our troubles. There was an undeniable magnetism between us that I hadn't felt in my prior relationships. Our long car rides to distant trailheads became more than mere drives. The hours we spent talking took our relationship to places I didn't know you could go. We continued these intimate talks on our hikes. John told me that one of his favorite quotes that was a mantra for his new life: "Life is either a daring adventure, or nothing." I felt the same way as both John and Helen Keller.

John spoke so passionately about his past life and his words hit home with me. We couldn't have met at a better time in our lives since we both faced the same challenges. Now we could dare to dream big dreams with a fellow dreamer. We realized that prioritizing our life goals was not only okay, but something that we needed to hold onto as we moved into the future. The shared purpose of our lives was seeking adventure, and we refused to let anyone else keep us from living rich lives.

# Chapter 24 – I Mean It This Time

After I told my family about my engagement to John, they were predictably torn asunder. Everyone wondered why I moved so fast; how could I still be married to Josh and engaged to John? They said, "You need at least two years after getting divorced to be ready to move on and start a new relationship." I explained that my divorce would be final on March 8, and that John and I planned a September wedding. I calmly told everyone to simmer down. It seemed laughable to me that I should spend another two years alone and recovering from my marriage. I had spent my life figuring out what I needed to do, and now was the time to move. I was in charge of my destiny, and I decided that two months was sufficient. These people didn't know my history, passion, or dreams. My heart screamed, "Yes," so I listened to its voice. The old Alyson might make decisions to please everyone else, but the new Alyson honored her heart.

I was barely involved in planning my first wedding. This time was different. I planned a dream wedding, and our passion for mountains was the obvious theme. John and I discussed where to hold the wedding and the answer was easy. We would get married on top of a mountain. We wanted the wedding in our favorite part of the state in September, our favorite month.

We decided to tie the knot in the San Juan Mountains on the rocky summit of Ulysses S. Grant Peak, the mountain we'd climbed the previous year. To complete the dream, we planned to spend our wedding night on the magical island in Island Lake below the peak. We planned to invite a few friends and family members to the summit ceremony and, for those unable to climb the peak, we would have a pre-wedding celebration in nearby Ouray.

We set the date for September 9, 2012. John and I designed the wedding invitation, which was titled: "JK & AK Wedding Time Adventures." Then, we listed options for people to choose their adventure:

# John and Alyson's Wedding Adventures

## Mini Adventure:

Adventure is right outside your door: Stay home, mail REI gift card to John and Alyson Kirk. This option includes an adventuresome walk to the mailbox!

## Splendid Adventure:

A traveling adventure of relaxation and fun: Partake in pre-wedding festivities. Meet on Saturday, September 8 at 3:00 p.m. on the Million Dollar Highway above Ouray for pictures and socializing, followed by dinner at Buen Tiempo. Indulge in some ice cream and sweets across the street after dinner and stay with the soon-to-be bride and groom at the Box Canyon Lodge, complete with mountainside hot spring pools to soak in the evening under a blanket of stars.

## Ultra Adventure:

An adventure for the outdoorsy person who's not afraid to get a little sweaty. Partake in the Splendid Adventure, but don't let the fun stop there. Let the fun begin! Sunday, September 9 at 5:30 a.m., depart from the hotel and go to the Mineral Creek Trailhead. There we will begin our three-and-a-half-mile backpacking hike to Ice Lake Basin with 2,000 feet of elevation gain. Spend the day relaxing at the lake and enjoying one of the most scenic places in the US. Set up camp, read, daydream, etc. Join the wedding party for dinner at the lake around 5:30 p.m. followed by dessert. For any drinkers in the bunch, please plan your own provisions!

## Mega Adventure:

A hair-raising, risk-taking, pee-your-pants adventure at its finest! Partake in the Splendid and Ultra Adventures, and then take the J & A wedding time adventures to the next level. After reaching Ice Lake and dropping off your overnight gear, grab your wedding attire, helmet, and harness. Climb to the summit of Ulysses S. Grant and watch John and Alyson become husband and wife on top of one of the most spectacular peaks in the state. This feat will not be easy; danger and risk of losing your life is included. Please allow some flexibility in your schedule in the event of inclement weather (wedding may potentially be delayed for up to a day). Please sign attached waiver if choosing this option. Also, consider wedding time adventures pre-training wedding camp to prepare for the big day - please review the attached training sheet.

We made the invitations lighthearted and had a blast with them. We invited 20 people, knowing that only a few would do the summit climb. We were fine if no one decided to climb the peak - we'd just marry ourselves on the summit. You can get married without anyone presiding over the ritual, so initially we thought we would do that. Later I invited Lynda and asked if she would perform the ceremony. Lynda agreed to attend and be our minister.

Since I'd met John, I didn't care what anyone thought about what I did. I wasn't worried about my dad anymore. I planned to be happy because of the choices I made without his support. If he loved me, he would want me to be happy. He may not accept my decisions or accept John as my husband; I wasn't going to wait for that to happen. I moved forward with my wedding plans. I would become Mrs. Kirk.


## Wedding Time!

John's parents bubbled with happiness after hearing that John and I were engaged, and I couldn't wait to have them as my in-laws. Time heals wounds, so most of my family had moved on from my divorce and accepted John. They saw that I was happy and that made them happy too.

My brother Daniel, his wife Meggie, my sister Sarah, her boyfriend Karl, and our good friends Molly, Susan, and Lynda joined us for the summit climb. The wedding was intimate with such a small group. The rest of our guests, including John's parents, my mom, my brother Kyle, and his girlfriend joined us in Ouray for the pre-wedding celebration.

We decided to create our own wedding ceremony and write our vows. We both worked diligently to make 2012 a special and unforgettable year.

Through it all, I grew close to John's mother. I could easily talk to Peggy. We called each other frequently and talked for hours. She was a skilled seamstress and could make almost anything out of cloth, so I asked her to make my wedding dress. She excitedly agreed. I was thrilled to have a handmade wedding dress to carry to the top of U. S. Grant for the summit ceremony. Peggy accepted me for who I was, encouraged me to do what I loved, and to be myself. She was happy that John and I were happy.

## Believers

As the wedding day approached, I was excited, nervous, and eager to become Mrs. Kirk. Our guests showed up for the weekend festivities in Ouray. We soaked at hot springs, enjoyed a fine Mexican dinner, and laughed at our mothers on the wedding photo shoot. They were afraid of heights and didn't enjoy the suspended walkway above the Uncompahgre River where the pictures were taken. They both crawled on hands and knees since they were too terrified to walk to the edge.

The day of my wedding finally arrived. We woke early, left the hot springs lodge, and drove to Mineral Creek Trailhead. I hoped everyone would do okay on the hike, but I fretted about the weather since there was a 40 percent chance of thunderstorms in the afternoon. I threw my hair up into something fancy, and found a flower near the trail for my hairdo.

We started hiking at 6:00 a.m., but the summit of U. S. Grant was almost 4,000 feet above us. John and I were used to scrambling up mountains, but I hoped the others could make it before the weather turned sour. We announced that if anyone had trouble with the peak climb, they should meet us for the post-wedding festivities at Island Lake.

The crisp air and cool breeze urged us upward on that beautiful September morning. Sunlight slanting through the pines promised a perfect day. We crossed below waterfalls, dodged cliffs, and huffed up steep switchbacks carrying heavy packs. John carried an iPod speaker box, climbing gear, ropes, a 25-dollar Walmart raft, food, and hung a rental tuxedo off his pack. I carried an assortment of gear and the handmade wedding dress. Finally, we reached Ice Lake Basin where the views opened in every direction. My family would camp here. The beauty of the alpine cirque blew them away.

To reach the lake, we hiked another half-mile to Island Lake at 12,400 feet where Ulysses S. Grant Peak loomed steeply over our heads. Daniel, Meggie, and Karl were exhausted and decided to stay at the lake with their dogs. I was excited that Daniel and Meggie, married two weeks earlier, had hiked up to the lake. We stashed the raft and camping gear on the lake shore, but the rent-a-tux and dress stayed with us.

It was time to head for the summit and the ceremony. We climbed a steep scree slope filled with slippery ball-bearing rocks to the high saddle between "V4" and U. S. Grant. With the sun shining on our ascent, everyone, except Sarah, enjoyed the scrambling ascent. John stashed his pack below the summit and ran up the final gully with the rent-a-tux draped over his shoulder flapping in his own breeze.

Our mood was light and spirited. I was excited to have Sarah, Lynda, and other friends with me. I noted a few dark clouds in the distance, but nothing to be concerned about yet. I went off one side of the summit to change into my dress, and John descended the opposite side to put on his tuxedo. When we were ready, Susan plugged an iPod into the speaker box and started our soundtrack. This was it.

With warm air, sunshine, and spacious views, John and I slowly walked toward each other to commit ourselves for the rest of our lives. John looked like a million dollars in his tuxedo. I had never seen him dressed up before, so it was good that I walked slowly since I couldn't take my eyes off him. There was no way I was going to stumble now.

This wedding was different than my first one. I knew that John was the love of my life, my soul-mate, and the man I wanted to be with forever.

When we reached each other, we clasped hands, and spontaneous tears filled my eyes. We stood and gazed into each other's eyes while Lynda read the ceremony. Next, we read our vows. I pulled my sacred sheet from a special fold in my dress. We honored the ancient adage of ladies first. I composed myself.

*John Derek Kirk, I love you with all my heart. I love you more than I knew was possible to love another human being.*

*You are my best friend. You are my lover. You are my soul-mate, and the one person put on this Earth just for me; there is no better match.*

*Today, I give myself to you in marriage. I promise to encourage and inspire you, to laugh with you, and to comfort you in times of sorrow and struggle. I promise to be unbalanced and do things in excess!*

*I will share in your dreams, and support you as you strive to achieve your goals. I will listen to you with compassion and understanding, and speak to you with encouragement.*

*I promise to trust in our growth, and our ability to change and discover new adventures together.*

*In all that life may bring us, my love is yours, forever.*

*Hand holding in the moonlight under starry skies, shining my headlamp in your face, smelling the flowers, all-nighters, 100-mile journeys, leg-shaking excitement, hair-raising lightning buzzing; the adventures and journeys have just begun!*

*These things I give to you today. And myself, I give you for life.*

I cried when John read his vows to me. His sweet, soft words were like a symphony dancing in my ears.

> *Alyson, you entered my life at a time when I had not known how to share my authentic self. Life had been about compromise and putting my dreams aside.*
>
> *You've shown me I can run farther than I ever imagined, dream bigger than I would have dared, and experience a happiness I never thought possible.*
>
> *You have shared with me the most profound love I have known. This was made possible through an undeniable connection between our intense personalities and deeply sharing each other's passions.*
>
> *You are my soul-mate, and will forever be my source of joy and excitement.*
>
> *Thank you for making this journey with me.*

As John read this, happy tears flushed my eyes. His words melted my heart and warmed my soul. They were the exact words that I hoped to hear one day, and I did, from the man I loved.

Just Married!

Now, it was heel-clicking time. The wedding ceremony was over and I was officially Mrs. Kirk. I was happy, in love, and on top of a mountain. We packed up and helped the wedding party down the mountain. The dark clouds stayed in the distance as we climbed down.

# Fantasy Island

After scuttling down the scree below the saddle, we arrived back at Island Lake where we met the rest of the wedding party. The weather was decent, so John and I decided we better test the cheesy Walmart raft to see if it could float us and our gear to the island without sinking. We hoped that our first adventure as a married couple wouldn't be a dunking in Island Lake's frigid water.

It's a fairytale to sail to a beautiful island for a wedding night. Now we were living the fantasy, but only if the raft worked. We inflated our boat and John gave it a test run. He loaded our packs, carefully sat in the remaining space, and pushed off with his ski poles. To save weight, we didn't bring a paddle, so John worked diligently with his skinny poles to cross the hundred yards to the island. He had a little trouble steering the snub-nosed contraption, but made it to the island without dunking the packs. He quickly set up the tent, then poled back to pick me up. We changed into matching wedding vests that John's mom had made us that said, "Just Married." I wobbled into our excuse for a raft, John got in behind me, and we paddled, or poled to our fantasy island dressed in Just Married attire. The moment felt surreal; this was really happening. The wedding party watched and waved as we paddled away.

Once camp was set up, we returned to the lakeshore to spend the rest of the evening with the others at their camp in lower Ice Lake Basin. This was the wedding reception. We hiked down to their camp and made everyone a feast of dehydrated camp food. We listened to music, talked, and visited. It was the best wedding I could have dreamed of. Some of the party enjoyed cocktails, while John and I sipped sparkling water.

Later that night, John and I sailed across Island Lake for our wedding night. We pulled the raft onto the island, turned it upside down, and tied it to rocks. We laughed when John attempted to carry me to the tent. There was no way he could actually carry me into the tiny tent, so we crawled inside.

Our island wedding night was a singular time that I'll never forget. The storm clouds finally moved across the mountains during the night, interrupting our dreams. Comfortable in our cocoon, we listened to hail batter the tent and wondered if it could pop the raft. Later the hail subsided to a gentle rain and we drifted into a dreamless married sleep.

## My First Day As Mrs. Kirk

We woke the next day with a honeymoon plan to climb nearby 13,380-foot South Lookout Peak. I didn't know much about the peak except that it was hard, dangerous, and one of the few remaining Thirteeners that John needed to climb in the area. We broke camp, poled across the lake, and hiked to Swamp Grant Pass above Island Lake. We headed east to the summit of "V 2," which we had climbed a year earlier. It was our first peak as a married couple. The real business of the day lay ahead of us.

13,380-foot South Lookout Peak
Photo by Gerry Roach

From the summit of "V 2," we saw the upper part of South Lookout. It looked scarier than I had imagined. With game faces on, we dropped into the upper end of Clear Lake Basin, then climbed over a high ridge to a descent and traverse to the peak. We climbed loose rock, crossed exposed ledges, and tip-toed along a narrow ridge. I let a few f-bombs escape.

I wondered why I was climbing this peak on my first day of marriage. If I was normal, I would probably be in a bubble bath painting my toenails or sitting on a beach getting sand in all the wrong places.

On the summit, my f-bombs morphed into shrieks of joy. This was my new life. I had married a man the day before who liked adventure and climbing as much as I did. I was a lucky woman. Tingling, I jumped into John's open arms.

We carefully down-climbed South Lookout trying to ignore the abyss below, then reversed our route back to Swamp Grant Pass. Here we could relax, looking smugly back at South Lookout and all the other peaks that we had already climbed.

We raced down to our packs above Island Lake and hefted them complete with wedding outfits and the inflatable raft. We passed the wedding party's Ice Lake Basin campsite, but they had already left. We had plans to treat everyone to dinner that night in Ouray, so we zipped back to the car.

Back in town, Daniel and Meggie let me have it. The nighttime storm had flooded their tents. They were drunk and it was dark so they packed up their stuff and made an intoxicated run down the trail to the parking lot. I eased their anger by buying them a good dinner and a round of drinks. I was in charge now.

My family was happy for me. They could tell that I was a different person, and that I had made tough decisions that led me to a happy place. I wasn't just happy, I was ecstatic, and my glow gave it away. They could tell that, as Mrs. Kirk, I was finally able to be my authentic self.

# Sky High Honeymoon

Our honeymoon started a few days after the wedding. We said goodbye to our families and friends, and hefted our packs without a wedding dress, rent-a-tux, and raft. This time we would sail away on our feet. John planned a sky-high agenda for a three-day, two-night backpacking trek into the remote and beautiful Weminuche Wilderness Area. We hoped to climb a dozen tough peaks including Peak Six, Peak Seven, Leviathan Peak, Vallecito Mountain, Storm King Peak, Peak Nine, and Mount Nebo.

We began by humping heavy packs over the summits of several Thirteeners, but the subsequent peak climbs were stunning. We camped along Vallecito Creek on the first night. The next morning, we reached an idyllic place at Lower Leviathan Lake, and set up shop there. No one else was around for miles. After invigorating ascents of Peak Nine and Storm King Peak, we retreated back to the campsite on the slope above the lake. Its still water reflected the towering peaks as well as us, making us part of the scene. A colorful sunset added to the beauty of the area. I felt that this was the most beautiful place I had ever visited.

John celebrated with a spontaneous cartwheel. Surrounded by beauty, mountains, and forest, we nuzzled together on the grass. The moment was perfection.

Photo by Alyson Kirk

# Chapter 25 – Doing The Unthinkable

Whizz…Smack! I tucked my head down as rocks careened down a gully. John and I were a hundred feet up a sloping pitch on Turret Ridge, one of Colorado's most difficult and dangerous peaks. Earlier that morning, lightning charged across the dark sky to reveal heavy cloud cover. We had already moved the climb ahead a day because of possible bad weather, and now we delayed our departure for an hour. The forecast called for sunshine later.

We hiked for two hours through rain on the approach, and then waited an hour to see if it cleared. It was an inauspicious start to the day. Rain had finally ended a few minutes earlier and a three-foot-high pile of graupel or corn snow at the bottom of the gully from the previous day's storm testified to the severe conditions. I peered up to check slack in the rope being pulled up. Occasionally the rope caught on protrusions and dislodged small stones and bounced them down my way.

I was anxious all night about this climb, and now found myself following John up the lower reaches of Turret Ridge. Teresa Gergen had first mentioned this peak to me during the recovery from my accident as I crutched around the park with her. I never imagined, however, that I would climb it, but here I was.

I had learned to doubt myself during childhood and then built upon that self-doubt as an adult. When I was a child, my father stood on the sidelines at sporting events and yelled how I was doing everything wrong. I never felt good enough. Now here I was dealing with doubt about my ability to climb this peak.

Would I spend the rest of my life letting other people cultivate more self-doubt? In the past, alcohol, drugs, and my eating disorder numbed me, tempering my emotions, and withdrawing into my self-doubt. After I quit alcohol and drugs, I took a big step toward battling self-doubt. However, eating disorders took the place of alcohol and drugs. I lived with my eating disorders for almost a decade. For years it seemed like suicide was a better option than fighting my disorders. That was my reality. I could spend the rest of my life battling eating disorders and self-doubt or I could overcome these issues.

As I belayed John above, I couldn't feel my fingers or toes in the wet 35-degree temperature. We wore every layer of clothes we brought, including puffy jackets and balaclavas, but were still racked with cold. Once I wouldn't have left the car in such poor weather for an easy peak and now here I was on one of the hardest peaks in extreme conditions. I had reservations, but tried to show confidence and believe in myself. The person I had become had more self-assurance than the person I once was.

When I reached the first belay stance, the air was frigid in the shadows of the vertical faces above, which blocked the morning sunlight. We climbed a short pitch and moved the belay to a higher ledge. The next lead worked up a vertical crack on the face to the left, passing a large chockstone or wedged boulder.

Turret Ridge, the highest point of a spiked rock ridge, offers a severe and committing climb on suspect rock, a loose volcanic tuff deposited by ancient eruptions. Turret Ridge wasn't ascended until 1979, when Colorado climbing legend Harvey T. Carter guided a party to the summit. Since his ascent, the route had seen fewer than 20 successful ascent parties.

The lead climber takes significant risks on Turret Ridge's upper pitches, with protection, like nuts and cams, difficult to find and with long run-outs on rotten terrain. One of the scariest pitches is the "Lichen Traverse," which I dreaded to follow.

John and I searched for someone to lead the route, but couldn't find anyone willing to take the risk. One promising person considered climbing with us, but said, "To be honest, my wife isn't excited at the idea of me going." We also asked a guiding company, but they said, "Honestly, it has been hard to get a guide interested in this objective. I suppose they don't find the risk is worth the reward." We had used a guide a few years before to lead us up Lizard Head Peak, the most challenging 13,000-foot summit in Colorado.

13,113-foot Lizard Head
Photo by Gerry Roach

We found the climbing on Lizard Head challenging, but it never felt dangerous. Its vertical pillar has seen hundreds of ascents, and while it has awful rock by climbing standards, it doesn't compare to Turret Ridge's dubious cobblestone and tuff walls.

Alyson climbing near Lizard Head's summit
Photo by John Kirk

The last ascent of Turret Ridge was less than a year earlier by friends Teresa Gergen and Kirk Mallory. Teresa is the only climber who has climbed it twice. John contacted their leader, but unfortunately, he was busy and unable to climb with us in the near future. As a last-ditch option, a climber recommended that John contact his friend in Durango about the route. He agreed to lead us, with a tone of optimism and confidence. We finally had a date on the calendar so this ascent just might happen.

The real climbing began in the first chimney, but it was easier and more enjoyable than it appeared. We had climbed during the past week at harder grades and our training appeared to be paying dividends. When I reached the top of the chimney, I took a moment to reflect on my long journey to this place.

John seconded the pitch as graupel began to fall, but the weather relented within a few minutes. Above, we quickly dispatched a roped scamper up a sloping grass slope. The next pitch is the technical crux of the climb, with a rating of Class 5.9. The climbing is difficult, and every hold feels like it's going to break off. Most unexpected, our leader took a 15-foot fall near the top of the pitch, swearing as he fell. John held him with a tight belay, and kept him from hitting a ledge below. The fall didn't help my sense of well-being. It appeared to us that our leader was okay after his fall, or so we thought.

Our leader said, "Let's try that again, and we'll assess from there." He continued climbing, placing camming devices in cracks and tying slings around chockstones. At the top of the pitch, he yelled, "Off belay!"

The first of two 100-foot chimneys mid-way up Turret Ridge
Photo by John Kirk

If our leader was going to keep climbing after his fall, I knew I had to try. There was no turning back; I couldn't give up. Then, it was my turn. The climbing looked impossible, and not long ago I would have retreated. I told myself I could do it. The climbing was hard and awkward. An overhanging section chewed up time, but rock climbing is often a battle of inches. Near the top of the pitch, light penetrated through the chimney, and it was clear that the chimney was not a crack in the formation, but rather a gap between two separate fins.

As I climbed, I thought about my past and how I wasn't going to let it dictate what I could do now. I had taken charge of my life and gained the confidence to do anything I wanted. Now, I was climbing Turret Ridge and nobody could stop me. Reaching this difficult summit was more to me than simply getting to the top of another peak. This ascent was a milestone of my growth and the woman I had become.

The view from the top of the upper chimney was the wildest thing I ever saw, but something prevented me from appreciating the view. The next section was the infamous "Lichen Traverse," and it had my undivided attention. The 50-foot horizontal traverse, while not difficult climbing, crosses a steep wall studded with lichen-covered cobbles. It looked more horrifying than I had imagined. To me, traverses are always scary and definitely in this case. I received a belay from both sides.

Our leader edged across the traverse before disappearing behind a corner. After attaching himself to the rock, he yelled that he was anchored. I collected my wits, and began moving from the safety of a ledge. A rush of air moved up the steep face, and snuck up my pants. I had never been in such a terrifying position, but I trusted my partners to keep me safe. More importantly, I trusted myself, and I knew I could climb this pitch. I went for it.

The hardest climbing, overhanging near the top
Photo by John Kirk

I moved across the section, and when I reached the anchor, yelled, "Oh, thank you, God!" John went last. He climbed across the traverse, and soon we saw him move around the corner. On his last two steps, both of John's handholds broke off the face. Thankfully, John was ok, but ended the traverse with bloody fingers. After that scary pitch, we knew we were going to reach Turret Ridge's summit.

The "Lichen Traverse" – Danger lives here
Photo by John Kirk

We scrambled up easy rock to the summit, and celebrated with a kiss. We placed a new register Teresa had given us with the names of all of the previous climbers that had been on the top. Standing atop the summit, tears of joy filled my eyes. I couldn't believe how far I had come on my journey. I felt grateful for my husband, for what we had just accomplished, and for the new life I had forged.

To descend, we made four rappels down the route. Rockfall was a constant threat as we descended the terrible rock. We reached the base of the route, and all three of us felt immediate relief. All that remained was descending a thousand feet of wooded slopes and a few miles to the car. We had done the scary stuff and reached the summit. We took off our rock-climbing shoes, and put trail running shoes back on. We coiled our ropes, collected our gear, and got our packs ready to go.

On the first few steps of our descent, we noticed that our leader was moving painfully slow. We went to him and asked what was going on. The problem was that he hit his ankle and foot hard during the fall earlier in the day. He didn't know that his ankle and foot were injured until he took off his tight-fitting climbing shoes, which appeared to have kept the swelling at bay during the rest of the climb. His ankle was now swollen, black and blue, and he could hardly walk. We weren't in a good place to be unable to walk. After being rescued myself, I knew I would do whatever it took to get him down the mountain.

My accident and rescue were at the forefront of my thoughts. I knew our situation wasn't as serious, but now it was my turn to help. I decided that I should pile all three packs, ropes, and everyone's gear on myself. With two packs on my back and one pack on my front, they were so heavy that I could hardly move. John assisted our leader, which included a few piggy-back rides down the mountain. We moved at a turtle's pace, but we were getting our leader down to safety. It felt good to help someone who was injured.

I finally went ahead, hustled down to our cars, dropped our packs, and ran to a nearby camp. I found a nice gentleman with an ATV, and told him about our predicament. I talked him into driving his ATV up an abandoned road to reach our friend and drive him down to the parking lot. He agreed and got our leader safely down the mountain. Our leader's obvious pain brought back memories of my pain I had during my rescue. After reaching the vehicles, we accessed our leader's injury. Luckily, it wasn't his driving foot. He said he would be ok to drive, and would head straight to the hospital to get checked out.

We said goodbye, and drove into the night. It wasn't long before we said, "Did we really just climb Turret Ridge? Did all of that really happen?" Oh my, what a day. So ended one of the most memorable days of my life.

12,260-foot Turret Ridge
Photo by Gerry Roach

# Postscript

We develop trivial passions and obsessions as children. Some kids ride a bike, play a sport, or get absorbed in video games. Some enthusiasts continue playing a sport throughout their life or become professional athletes. Maybe the video game player becomes a high-profile IT specialist. Passions evolve as we age, fade away if not nurtured, or take on a more passive role. Passions take a back seat to daily roles and responsibilities, and we sometimes become spectators, fulfilling our craving for adventure and discovery vicariously. Sometimes we become consumers rather than producers of experience by watching television, movies, or sports. It's easy to lose the thrill of adventure, especially if we think we're not good enough at something. Our life becomes stressful and complicated, and we don't make the time to pursue our passions among our family and work responsibilities. We settle for our experiences rather than prioritizing them.

It is less common that someone cultivates and thrives on their passion for life. Your adult passions may not have anything to do with childhood interests, but the passion has always been there - it's hard-wired in humans. For some of us, we depend on it. Some people turn to alcohol and drugs in an attempt to mask the raw experiences that are missing from their lives.

Somewhere along our journey, we may learn to doubt our abilities and abandon our potential. In our earliest ambitions, we believe we can be something great, because we see and hear great stories of others. As we grow up this belief shrinks and sometimes disappears. Some children, future Olympians for example, channel it. They are talented, nurtured, and encouraged with a support system. This is not usually the case for most of us. Over time, we hear voices telling us we can't or shouldn't or won't. We hear these voices more than the ones which say we can or will. We live in a pattern where we often think we're not capable of something, and we then seek familiarity and homeostasis. We stick with what's comfortable. It is uncomfortable to challenge our self-concept.

Of course, we can't be anything and everything. Climbing mountains isn't for everyone, and while metaphoric and symbolic in overcoming adversity, so are all challenges we are willing to face to redefine our self-perception. To do remarkable things, we have to discover our motivations and develop and cultivate our passions.

I will always challenge myself in the future to experience remarkable and extraordinary things. I do not see a future for me to never challenge myself to experience or achieve something I overcame much in my life, despite having the odds stacked against me. I defeated addictions to alcohol and drugs and overcame a life-threatening eating disorder. I graduated from college with an MBA and now I own and operate a successful small business. I ran when others said I couldn't run. I climbed when others said I couldn't climb. I followed my heart and believed in what I wanted. I proved to myself that I am who I strive to be. When you believe in yourself, despite how the outside world shapes and defines you, you allow the remarkable and extraordinary to happen.

Now I don't drink, smoke, or use drugs. My weight is under control, and I'm fit and healthy. I have my own financial security. I'm madly in love with John, my soul-mate. To date, I've finished fourteen 100-mile runs, along with many 100k's (64.2miles) and 50-mile ultra-marathons. I won the Grand Mesa 100 in 2014. I won the Zion 100 in 2017 while struggling with the flu. I won the Lonestar 100 in Texas in February, 2018. Two months later I won the Hellbender 100 in North Carolina, then won the Cloudsplitter 100 in Virginia in October, 2018. I won Colorado's Never Summer 100k three consecutive years (2014-2017). On September 17, 2017 I became the second woman and youngest person in history to complete climbing the 1,313 peaks in Colorado above 12,000 feet.

The things that I have completed are beyond my earlier dreams. Earlier in my life, even considering these goals was beyond my wildest of ambitions. Most importantly, I try to live authentically every day. This is the person I was all along. It just took me a long time to discover her.

John and I seek adventure every chance we get. We are rarely home on weekends, and spend more nights camping outside than we do sleeping in a bed. John and I climbed over 500 peaks together in the fall of 2011, and we've each climbed over 1,000 peaks every year since. I was with John when he finished Colorado's Thirteeners, and all 1,313 of Colorado's peaks above 12,000 feet. John was with me when I finished Colorado's Thirteeners, and all 1,313 of Colorado's peaks above 12,000 feet, repeating many of these peaks with me to help me attain this goal. John and I also run 100-mile ultra-marathons together. The key word is "together." We live together and do what we love together - sharing our mountain passion and experiences.

In the fall of 2017, after completing the 1,313-peak goal, I was interviewed on television for my achievement. I made radio appearances and appeared in a few magazines. I was featured in a 2017 Elevation Outdoors magazine article, "Colorado Badassess." I've been interviewed in podcasts specific to ultra-running. I've had numerous people contact me through social media to let me know that I've been an inspiration.

We plan to climb mountains for the rest of our lives. In fact, our summit goals continue to entail more daring and wild dreams than ever before. Goal-setting is a vital part of who we are and who we will become. Our long-term goal, well underway, has been dubbed "The Kirk Project" - to reach the summit of every peak above 12,000 feet in the contiguous United States. No one has dared to take on this challenge, let alone view it as achievable. There are over 2,100 peaks meeting the mark, with much of the list in some of the most remote and rugged wilderness in the Western US. A project of this duration and magnitude will certainly test our perseverance, skill, and dedication. We very well may not succeed, but we will not abandon the goal. It is the journey and process in overcoming adversity that is the fulfillment in seeing the goal through.


Why did I want to write a book? I've had a rough life. Obviously not as rough as some other people's lives, but I've been through serious struggles and overcome most of them. I know the future will bring more challenges, and I'm ready for them. I believe that my story provides inspiration to others with struggles like mine. Some struggles are life-altering, some are life-shattering, and some are fatal. You don't have to have a near-death experience to make drastic changes in life. I had one such experience, and the changes I vowed to make at the time proved to be difficult. Perhaps if I did not have a near-death experience on Rosalie Peak, I wouldn't have had such deep introspection or courage to make serious life changes. I thought there was no one I could turn to for help. I was wrong. You can always find caring people willing to help you recover and grow. My fear of failure and lack of self-esteem could have destroyed me, but I found incredible strength the night I faced death in a blizzard on Rosalie Peak. Perhaps it is true that we don't know how strong we are until being strong is our only choice.

I know I will always struggle with my eating disorder, but I also know that I have the upper hand. I've had fewer relapses, and it's been over three years since my last slip into bulimia. I learned the triggers for the self-destructive behavior. I took frustrations and anger out on myself. I've taken my passions to the extreme and with each mountain I climb and each race I run, I give myself the confidence and sense of self-worth that I was missing.

Not everyone wants to be a climber or runner. What matters is that you take an honest look at yourself and accept who you are, and know that you can't go through life pretending to be someone else. It's important to embrace your passions and make them a priority. There is no substitute for working on your own happiness. You must believe in yourself and make smart choices, and know that you have a purpose in the journey of life.

I believe our past doesn't define our future. With that said, if my father were to accept me, John, and a future relationship, I would accept. I know it would take a lot of work; great things take hard work in life. Whether it be finishing a list of peaks, having a strong marriage, or raising kids. My father lost his twin brother at an early age, and part of me feels that this has affected him emotionally with relationships ever since. I love you Dad. No matter how bad things have been, I'm more than capable and fine with living the rest of my life without you, I just hope that I don't have to. The choice is yours.

I hope that this book might inspire or help just one person to break free of the self-imposed chains that hold us back in life - to make the decisions enabling a better path in life. A frightful childhood shouldn't condemn you to a life of misery. The mistakes you make as a teenager or young adult shouldn't define you. We all deserve happiness. Again, there are so many wonderful people who will help us overcome some of our life struggles if we let them. My story is full of those people.

Is this a fairy tale ending for me where everyone lives happily ever after? No, but I think it's as close as it gets!

Made in the USA
Columbia, SC
17 January 2019